Costly Policies

Costly Policies

State Regulation and Antitrust Exemption in Insurance Markets

Jonathan R. Macey and Geoffrey P. Miller

The AEI Press

Publisher for the American Enterprise Institute
WASHINGTON, D.C.

1993

368
M 142

Distributed by arrangement with

University Press of America, Inc.

| 4720 Boston Way | 3 Henrietta Street |
| Lanham, Md. 20706 | London WC2E 8LU England |

Library of Congress Cataloging-in-Publication Data

Macey, Jonathan R.
    Costly policies : state regulation and antitrust exemption in insurance markets /
Jonathan R. Macey and Geoffrey P. Miller.
        p.   cm.—(AEI studies in regulation and federalism)
    Includes bibliographical references.
    ISBN 0-8447-3831-X (cloth).—ISBN 0-8447-3830-1 (pbk.)
        1. Insurance—United States—State supervision.   2. Insurance law—United
States.   3. Antitrust law—United States.   I. Miller, Geoffrey P.
II. Title. III. Series.
HG8535.M27   1993
368'.973—dc20   93-15355
                                                                                CIP

1 3 5 7 9 10 8 6 4 2

THE AEI PRESS
Publisher for the American Enterprise Institute
1150 Seventeenth Street, N.W., Washington, D.C. 20036

Printed in the United States of America

Contents

Foreword

JONATHAN R. MACEY and Geoffrey P. Miller's study of the antitrust exemption for insurance markets is one of a series of research monographs commissioned by the American Enterprise Institute's Regulation and Federalism Project. The purpose of the project is to examine the advantages and disadvantages of American federalism in important areas of contemporary business regulation, including product labeling, advertising, insurance, transportation, communications, and environmental quality.

The benefits of state autonomy—diversity, responsiveness to local circumstances, and constraint on the power of the national government—are fundamental to the American political creed and deeply embedded in our political institutions. Are these benefits real and substantial in the case of business regulation? How do they compare with the costs of duplication, inconsistency, and interference with free interstate commerce that state regulation can entail? Has the growth of national and international commerce altered the balance of federalism's benefits and costs—for example, by affecting the ability of individual states to pursue local policies at the expense of citizens of other states? Are there practical means of reducing the economic costs of state autonomy in regulation while preserving its political benefits?

The authors of these volumes have found different answers to these questions in the context of different market and regulatory regimes: they call for greater national uniformity in some cases, greater state autonomy in others, and a revision of the rules of state "policy competition" in still others. We hope that this research will be useful to officials and legislators at all levels of government and to the business executives who must live with their policies. More generally, we hope that the AEI project will prove to be a significant contribution to our understanding of one of the most distinctive and important features of American government.

Each of the monographs produced for the Regulation and Federalism Project was discussed and criticized at an AEI seminar involving federal and state lawmakers, business executives, professionals, and academic experts with a wide range of interests and viewpoints. I would like to thank all of them for their contributions, noting, however, that the final exposition and conclusions were entirely the work of the authors of each monograph. I am particularly grateful to Jonathan R. Macey of Cornell University and Heather Gradison of AEI, who organized and directed the project's research and seminars along with me, and to John D. Ong and Jon V. Heider of the BFGoodrich Company and Patricia H. Engman of the Business Roundtable, who suggested the project in the first place, worked hard and effectively to raise financial support for it, and provided valuable counsel and encouragement throughout.

CHRISTOPHER C. DeMUTH
President, American Enterprise Institute
for Public Policy Research

1
Introduction

AMONG MAJOR FINANCIAL institutions in the United States, only insurance firms are subject to plenary state regulation. Not only has the federal government eschewed regulation, but it has affirmatively declared a policy of *not* regulating the business of insurance. This is so even though the U.S. insurance industry is the largest in the world, receiving $431 billion in premium income in 1988, an amount that represents 37 percent of the total insurance premium volume worldwide.[1]

The policy against regulating insurance is found in the McCarran-Ferguson Act,[2] which provides, in pertinent part, that "the business of insurance, and every person engaged therein, shall be subject to the laws of the several States which relate to the regulation or taxation of such business."[3] The act declares that "the continued regulation and taxation by the several States of the business of insurance is in the public interest, and . . . silence on the part of the Congress shall not be construed to impose any barrier to the regulation or taxation of such business by the several States."[4] Further, "no Act of Congress shall be construed to invalidate, impair, or supersede any law enacted by any State for the purpose of regulating the business of insurance, or which imposes a fee or tax upon such business, unless such Act specifically relates to the business of insurance."[5]

With respect to the federal antitrust laws, the statute provides, somewhat ambiguously, that the Sherman Act, the Clayton Act, and

---

[1]See Insurance Information Institute, *Insurance Facts* (Washington, D.C., 1991).

[2]15 U.S.C. § 1011–1015.

[3]15 U.S.C. § 1012(a).

[4]15 U.S.C. § 1011.

[5]15 U.S.C. § 1012(b).

1

the Federal Trade Commission Act apply to the business of insurance "to the extent that such business is not regulated by State law."[6] Notwithstanding the presence of state legislation, however, the statute provides that the Sherman Act shall apply to "any agreement to boycott, coerce, or intimidate, or act of boycott, coercion, or intimidation."[7] Also applicable to the insurance industry, despite the presence of state regulation, are a number of other statutes: the National Labor Relations Act, the Fair Labor Standards Act, and the Merchant Marine Act.[8]

The McCarran-Ferguson Act is unusual—perhaps unique—in the extraordinary degree of deference it displays toward state regulation. Many federal statutes implement mixed systems of regulations in which states are given a prominent role. But few, if any, other statutes expressly assign the states exclusive regulatory jurisdiction over an area of commerce or so clearly disavow the value of federal regulation.

The pattern in the insurance industry is particularly remarkable when we compare it with that of its near relatives such as the banking and securities industries. Here state and federal regulation commingle. For the most part, however, the federal regulatory presence predominates both industries. And the trend in these industries has been toward ever more federal control. The securities industry was essentially unregulated at the federal level until 1933;[9] but since then Congress, the courts, and the Securities and Exchange Commission (SEC) have steadily increased the stringency of federal oversight, to the point where state "blue sky" securities laws have been reduced to the role of supporting actors in the regulatory drama.[10] Banking

---

[6]Ibid.

[7]15 U.S.C. § 1013(b).

[8]15 U.S.C. § 1014.

[9]See Jonathan R. Macey and Geoffrey P. Miller, "Origin of the Blue Sky Laws," *Texas Law Review*, vol. 70 (1991), p. 347.

[10]Important federal securities statutes include the Securities Act of 1933, the Securities Exchange Act of 1934, the Public Utilities Holding Company Act of 1935, the Trust Indenture Act of 1939, the Investment Company Act of 1940, and the Investment Advisors Act of 1940. Congress has also adopted a variety of more recent, if less fundamental, revisions to these statutes. See, generally, L. Loss and J. Seligman, *Securities Regulation*, vol. 1, 3d ed. (Boston: Little Brown & Co., 1989), pp. 226–27.

has also witnessed a steady enhancement of federal regulatory power, although the process here began much earlier, with the creation of a system of national banks in the Banking Act of 1863. The process of regulatory nationalization continued apace through the twentieth century, however, with the enactment of many pieces of important legislation. At this writing, Congress has enacted yet another fundamental overhaul of banking industry regulation.[11] These statutes or administrative actions are often coupled with express preemptions of state regulatory power.[12]

Although anomalous, the insurance industry's exemption from federal regulation was not particularly controversial until the 1980s. Recently, however, the liability insurance crisis of the mid-1980s[13] and the failures of several major insurance companies in 1991 have sparked renewed interest in the McCarran-Ferguson Act, much of it critical.[14] Members of Congress held hearings[15] and introduced

---

[11]Federal Deposit Insurance Corporation Improvement Act of 1991, Pub. L. No. 102–242, 105 Stat. 2236. See Jonathan R. Macey and Geoffrey P. Miller, "America's Banking System: The Origins and Future of the Current Crisis," *Washington University Law Quarterly*, vol. 69 (1991), p. 769.

[12]See Henry Butler and Jonathan R. Macey, "The Myth of Competition in the Dual Banking System," *Cornell Law Review* (1988), p. 101.

[13]During this time, especially in 1985 and 1986, liability insurance rates skyrocketed across the country, and, in some cases, insurance became unavailable altogether. Particularly hard hit were school boards, municipalities, charities, and smaller businesses—groups that quickly voiced their dissatisfaction with the situation in the political process.

[14]These included the collapse of the Executive Life Insurance Companies of California and New York, the thirty-third and eighty-fifth largest firms in the North American life insurance industry with $10.2 billion and $3.2 billion in admitted assets, respectively, and the failure of Mutual Benefit Life Insurance Company, the twenty-first largest firm in the industry with $13.8 billion in admitted assets. Also raising public concern was the failure of Monarch Capital, the parent of Monarch Life Insurance Co., the sixty-sixth largest firm in the North American life insurance industry with $4.5 billion in admitted assets. See Susan Pulliam, "Mutual Benefit Life Is Expected to Ask State to Take Over as Early as Today," *Wall Street Journal*, July 15, 1991; "Life & Health Statistical Review," *National Underwriter*, June 10, 1991, p. S3.

[15]See H.R. 9, *The Insurance Competitive Pricing* Act of 1991, Economic and Commercial Law Subcommittee of the House Judiciary Committee, June 13, 1991 (prepared statements on file with the authors) (hereafter H.R. 9 Hearings).

legislation[16] to overturn the antitrust exemption.[17] The General

[16]See H.R. 9, 102d Congress, 1st session (1991) (introduced by Rep. Brooks); S. 430, 102d Congress, 1st session (1991) (introduced by Sen. Metzenbaum). H.R. 9 was reported out of subcommittee on November 14, 1991, and out of the full House Judiciary Committee (with amendments) on November 19, 1991. There has been no action on the bill since. Meanwhile, chances for a compromise on the legislation appear to be dimming; in late May 1992 the powerful National Association of Professional Insurance Agents resolved to oppose H.R. 9 because of its adverse effects on independent insurance agents. See "Compromise Isn't Imminent on Bill to Alter McCarran-Ferguson Exemption," BNA Antitrust and Trade Regulation Report, vol. 62 (June 11, 1992), p. 757. The Antitrust Division of the Department of Justice, while advocating review of the McCarran-Ferguson Act's antitrust exemption, nevertheless opposes H.R. 9 as having an "unwarranted deterrent effect on appropriate collective activity among insurers." Ruth Gastel, Antitrust, Insurance Information Institute (Washington, D.C., April 1992).

[17]The political forces favoring repeal of the antitrust exemption are now powerful and well organized, including in their number the National Association of Attorneys General, major consumer groups, the commercial banking industry (which is seeking entry into insurance markets), and others. See Statement of George W. Sampson, assistant attorney general of New York, in H.R. 9 Hearings; Statement of J. Robert Hunter, president, National Insurance Consumer Organization, in H.R. 9 Hearings. Important general periodicals have also begun to weigh in against the antitrust exemption. See, for example, "Bust the Insurance Cartel," New York Times, May 4, 1991; "End McCarran-Ferguson," Journal of Commerce, May 25, 1988; "The Insurance Cartel Is Ripe for Busting," Business Week, April 11, 1988.

As of the present writing, groups opposing repeal of the antitrust exemption include, among others, the Alliance of American Insurers, the American Council of Life Insurance, the Health Insurance Association of America, the National Association of Independent Insurers, the National Association of Life Companies, the National Association of Mutual Insurance Companies, and the National Association of Life Underwriters. See Statement of S. Roy Woodall, Jr., in H.R. 9 Hearings; Longo, "Changes to Come," Financial Services Week, June 24, 1991.

The insurance industry has traditionally presented a united front against any efforts to repeal or weaken the antitrust exemption. Recently, however, some strains have appeared within the industry itself. Some individual industry leaders have even expressed the view that their firms do not need the protection of the McCarran-Ferguson Act. See, for example, Richard L. Hall, "If Solvency Is a Problem, Is Federal Regulation the Solution," Best's Review, vol. 91, no. 10 (1991), p. 108 (reporting remarks of Caleb Fowler, president of CIGNA Property & Casualty Companies).

The current movement to repeal or modify the antitrust exemption can perhaps be dated from the Report of the National Commission for the Review of Antitrust Laws and Procedures (1979), pp. 225–51, which recommended repeal of the McCarran-Ferguson Act's broad antitrust immunity and its replacement by "narrowly drawn legislation . . . to affirm the lawfulness of a limited number of essential collective activities under the antitrust laws." See also Paul MacAvoy, ed., Federal-State

Accounting Office (GAO)[18] and powerful congressional committees[19] have criticized the way in which state regulators handle financially troubled insurers, and proposals have been aired in both houses of Congress to subject the insurance industry to federal regulatory oversight.[20] Others have called for the establishment of a presidential commission to study the industry's problems.[21]

Meanwhile, developments outside Washington, D.C., have also altered the political situation. Several states—most notably California, New Jersey, and Texas—began to impose much more stringent regulations on the insurance industry.[22] Insurance rate setting be-

Regulation of the Pricing and Marketing of Insurance (Washington, D.C.: American Enterprise Institute, 1977), an influential earlier study favoring market mechanisms for rate setting.

[18]See these reports from the General Accounting Office: *Insurance Regulation: State Handling of Financially Troubled Property/Casualty Insurers* (1991); *Insurance Regulation: Assessment of the National Association of the Insurance Commissioners* (testimony before the Subcommittee on Oversight and Investigations of the House Energy and Commerce Committee, 1991); *Questions and Concerns about Solvency Regulation* (1991); *Problems in State Monitoring of Property/Casualty Insurer Solvency* (1989).

[19]See *Failed Promises: Insurance Company Insolvencies*, Report by the Subcommittee on Oversight and Investigations of the Committee on Energy and Commerce (1990). Very recently the Subcommittee on Commerce, Consumer Protection, and Competitiveness of the House Energy and Commerce Committee held hearings on insurance solvency (July 17, 1991) and on life insurance guaranty funds (July 24, 1991) during which the performance of state solvency regulations came under sharp attack.

[20]See Frederick Rose, "Congressional Proposals on Insurance Would End Primacy of State Regulation," *Wall Street Journal*, August 5, 1991 (bills introduced by Senator Howard Metzenbaum and Congressman John Dingell). Opponents of federal insurance regulation have established an umbrella organization, the Coalition against Federal Regulation of Insurance, which includes state regulatory authorities as well as industry interests. See Statement of S. Roy Woodall, Jr., in H.R. 9 Hearings.

[21]See S. 1276, Presidential Insurance Commission Act (102d Cong., 1st session); Mary Jane Fisher, "Dodd Proposes Presidential Commission on Ins.," *National Underwriter*, June 24, 1991.

[22]California required a rollback of insurance rates and applied its antitrust law to insurance regulation in 1988 as a result of a ballot referendum (Proposition 103). In June 1991, Texas enacted major insurance reform legislation, the Omnibus Insurance Reform Bill of 1991, which, among other things, strengthened solvency requirements, established an office of public insurance counsel to represent consumers in insurance rate-setting proceedings, and repealed the insurance

came a burden rather than a boon to the industry in several states. A number of states have repealed their "mini-McCarran-Ferguson acts," which exempted the business of insurance from state antitrust laws, and others have begun to enforce their state antitrust laws with greater vigor. In May 1991, the U.S. Court of Appeals for the Ninth Circuit issued an important decision expansively interpreting the boycott exception to the McCarran-Ferguson Act,[23] thus applying the Sherman Act far more broadly than many in the insurance industry had believed possible. These developments have considerably reduced the perceived value of the antitrust exemption for many insurance companies. They have also contributed to a fracturing of the united industry front that until recently opposed any attempt to scale back the exemption.

These recent events suggest the potential value of a comprehensive review of the McCarran-Ferguson Act's pattern of regulatory federalism. This volume attempts such a reevaluation. Our major conclusions are these:

1. *The antitrust exemption should be interpreted in such a way as to allow vigorous enforcement against industry practices that threaten competition, while permitting efficiency-enhancing cooperative activities in the areas of information sharing and analysis and the development of standardized forms.*

The goal of antitrust regulation of the insurance industry should be to preserve and enhance competitive forces. The McCarran-Ferguson Act should be interpreted to permit vigorous enforcement against industry practices that suppress or threaten to suppress competition. Thus, a relatively expansive interpretation of the boycott exception to the act is indicated. Similarly, state action immunity should be limited to situations in which the activities in question are both endorsed by express state legislation or regulation, and not merely permitted as a matter of administrative practice or authorized by implication, and subject to active, continuous, and meaningful state oversight.

At the same time, however, the insurance industry is subject to

---

industry's exemption from the state antitrust laws. New Jersey enacted legislation in 1990 to roll back automobile insurance rates.

[23]In re Insurance Antitrust Litigation, 938 F.2d 919 (9th Cir. 1991), cert. granted sub nom. Hartford Fire Insurance Co. v. California, 113 S.Ct.52 (1992).

special economic problems that do not affect other industries to the same extent. In particular, casualty and liability insurance firms need to be able to share loss information in order to facilitate accurate pricing of insurance products. Cooperative efforts at sharing and analyzing historical loss cost information should be protected against antitrust scrutiny. Similarly, accurate information cannot be developed—and consumers cannot easily comparison shop on the basis of price—unless firms in the industry have access to standardized forms. Cooperative efforts to develop standardized forms should be protected against antitrust scrutiny, although efforts to coerce insurers to use any particular form or forms should be subject to scrutiny under the boycott exception to the act.

In general, recent interpretations of the McCarran-Ferguson Act have adopted a reasonable construction of the statute. Thus, we do not believe that the act is now in need of fundamental modification or repeal. If, however, the statute receives a judicial construction that interferes with the power of the federal antitrust laws to police against threats to competition within the industry, we would then recommend that Congress consider legislation to provide explicit safe harbors for economically efficient cooperative activities that do not pose serious threats to competition—such as the sharing and cooperative analysis of historical loss data and the cooperative development of standardized forms.

2. *Solvency regulation should generally be left to the states, but the Federal Reserve Board should be available as lender of last resort.* No convincing evidence shows that state solvency regulation is fatally flawed or that federal solvency regulation would be better than the existing system. Despite a few recent failures, the level of insolvencies of insurance firms has been extraordinarily low. There is little evidence, moreover, that insurance companies are failing because of lax supervision. For the most part, recent failures have been the result of unforeseeable downturns in real estate and corporate debt markets—systemic developments that have affected all financial services industries. What is remarkable is not that insurance companies are failing but that so few have failed in the volatile markets of the 1980s and 1990s.

Even if state insurance departments have exercised insufficient scrutiny over some companies in recent years, this lapse is hardly a compelling reason to support preemptive federal regulation. State insurance regulators are moving rapidly to increase the stringency of their solvency regulations. Moreover, the federal government has certainly not acquitted itself well in the analogous field of banking regulation, where the largest financial catastrophe in the history of the United States is now under way, partly as a result of inadequate regulatory supervision by federal banking agencies. Compared with the banking industry, which is heavily regulated at the federal level, the insurance industry, with plenary state regulation, is a stunning success story. After a century and a half of successful state regulation, there are no persuasive arguments for federal solvency regulation at this time.[24]

We believe, however, that there is a limited role for the federal government in solvency regulation, in that a lender of last resort should be available to assist solvent insurance companies faced with policyholder runs, such as that which occurred to Mutual Benefit Life, or with sudden systemic demands on the assets of property and casualty firms as a result of a major disaster, such as a major earthquake. The logical candidate for such a lender of last resort would be the Federal Reserve Board, which already performs a similar function for the banking industry. We emphasize, however, that temporary liquidity assistance from the Federal Reserve should be provided only to insurance firms believed to be solvent and should be advanced only on a fully collateralized basis. An extensive insurance industry call on the Federal Reserve for liquidity loans is unlikely, but the advantages of temporary liquidity assistance are sufficiently great to warrant the establishment of a lender-of-last-resort facility for the insurance industry.

3. *Rates should be set by market forces.* Regulation of insurance premiums yields rates that are too high or too low, produces distortions and shortages, harms both consumers and producers, and requires costly government enforcement efforts to boot. In the absence of government control or private cartelization, marketplace forces would function effectively to set rates at optimal levels in this highly competitive, unconcentrated industry.

The public policy arguments in favor of free-market rate setting

---

[24]See American Bar Association, *Report of the Commission to Improve the Liability Insurance System* (1989), p. 10: "The tradition of state regulation, the long-standing experience shared by the state insurance agencies, and the adjustment of the industry to state regulatory requirements should not be discarded lightly."

are compelling. Over the past twenty years, the trend in the states has been to allow greater use of free-market rate setting, with results beneficial to insurance consumers. We hope that this trend will continue.

Recently, however, several states have returned to, or considered returning to, state-controlled rates in one form or another. Moreover, in an especially troubling development, several states now impose penalties or "exit taxes" on insurance firms that decide to leave a given state rather than comply with rate regulations that the firm finds onerous. The "lock-in" rules undermine long-standing market-place checks against state expropriation of insurance industry assets. In the long run, they may well harm consumers (by reducing the supply of insurance), undermine industry solvency, and spark an unhealthy competition in which states vie to set rates unrealistically low to benefit their own citizens at the expense of the national interest.

As yet, the trend back to administrative rate setting is not yet so pronounced as to suggest the need for preemptive federal regulation invalidating state rate regulation.[25] The problem of exit fees, however, is serious enough to warrant a limited preemption to prohibit states from penalizing any firm that elects to leave a state's market, or to leave any line of insurance within a state's market, when the firm's decision is based on economic cost factors and is not part of any boycott or collusion to pressure the state to alter or amend its regulations.

The important virtues of federalism do not indicate deference to state action in this context. From the standpoint of public policy, there is little justification for allowing states to trap insurance firms within their borders when the firms want to leave. If states could capture insurance firms by imposing onerous exit fees, the effect would be to detract from federalism values, since the consequence would be to remove one of the principal mechanisms by which corporations are protected against expropriative or excessively burdensome legislation at the state level.

This volume is structured as follows. Chapter 2 examines the general pattern of regulatory federalism for the insurance industry.

---

[25]Whether such legislation could be passed is another question; given the popularity of state rate rollbacks, we doubt that it would have much chance in any event.

Chapter 3 analyzes the antitrust exemption under the McCarran-Ferguson Act. Chapter 4 considers the application of the McCarran-Ferguson Act outside the antitrust area and assesses the argument for continued state solvency regulation. Chapter 5 evaluates the pros and cons of rate regulation. Our findings are summarized briefly in the conclusion, chapter 6.

2

Regulatory Federalism
in Insurance

BEFORE TREATING THE APPLICATION of the McCarran-Ferguson Act specifically to antitrust, solvency, and rate regulation, we outline the dynamics of regulatory federalism within the insurance industry under the statute. We examine the coverage issue—what is the scope of the "business of insurance"—and then consider three situations in which federal law might apply to activities falling within the business of insurance: where the state has not regulated the activity in question, where Congress has preempted state regulation, and where the state regulation would violate the federal Constitution. Finally, we evaluate several different models of regulation under the McCarran-Ferguson Act.

The "Business of Insurance"

The scope of the statute is determined by the meaning of the somewhat vague phrase the *business of insurance*.[1] A particular activity, even if undertaken by an insurance company, is not protected from federal regulation if it is not within the scope of the business of insurance. We look first at possible interpretations of the phrase and then consider the relevant judicial decisions.

Possible Interpretations. The McCarran-Ferguson Act provides an exemption only for the "business of insurance." That phrase, however, is left undefined and is subject to a relatively wide range of

---

[1]For a collection of the cases, see Annot., Validity, Construction, and Application of McCarran-Ferguson Act (15 U.S.C. §§ 1011–15), Dealing With Regulation of Insurance Business by State or Federal Law, 21 L.Ed. 2d 938 (Rochester, N.Y.: Lawyers Coop/Bancroft-Whitney, 1990).

possible interpretations, including the following:

1. The *business of insurance* means only the actual contract of insurance by which risk is passed from the policyholder to the insurance company. All other aspects of the insurance enterprise— for example, the process by which the insurance company lays off risk in reinsurance markets—are outside the definition. This is the narrowest possible reading, but it is not an implausible one. The passing of risk from insured to insurer is clearly at the core of the insurance enterprise. It was concerted activity by the fire insurance industry with respect to premium rates in the core insurance contract that triggered the prosecutions in the *South-Eastern Underwriters Association* case[2] and that led directly to the passage of the McCarran-Ferguson Act. Given this historical background and the functional importance of the basic insurance contract between provider and customer, it could plausibly limit the business of insurance to this core activity.

2. A somewhat broader approach would include within the term *business of insurance* all activities regularly conducted by firms that have as their principal purpose and effect the passage of risk from one party to another. This interpretation, which addresses the basic economic function of insurance, would bring within the business of insurance activities such as reinsurance, as well as nontraditional contracts with customers (such as some types of annuities), so long as they have the purpose and effect of passing risk. The passage of risk, however, would have to be the principal reason for the transaction. Virtually all commercial transactions of any complexity carry with them some allocation of risks between the parties, and the term *business of insurance* could not possibly cover all transactions in which some risk is transferred without sweeping virtually all commerce within the scope of the McCarran-Ferguson Act. Ordinary commercial transactions in which some risk is transferred may have an insurance feature, but they are not part of the "business" of insurance.

3. Somewhat more expansive still is an approach that includes not only transactions with the transfer of risk as their principal purpose and effect but also other transactions that, while not them-

---

[2]United States v. South-Eastern Underwriters Association, 322 U.S. 533 (1944).

12

selves involving the transfer of risk, are directly related to the function of transferring risk. The relations between an insurance company and its agents, for example, do not themselves usually involve the transfer of risk as their principal feature. Yet without agents, insurance that does transfer risk could not easily be sold. Agency contracts, together with a variety of other transactions by insurance companies, would fall within the category of transactions directly related to the function of transferring risk.

4. Finally, perhaps the most expansive interpretation of the term *business of insurance* would include not only transactions directly related to the transfer of risk but also all activities generally and traditionally engaged in by insurance companies. Investment functions such as the making of loans and the purchase of securities, for example, would be included, as well as all sorts of other functions necessary or convenient to the activities of a specialized risk bearer.

Judicial Decisions. It is not always clear which of these interpretations (if any) correctly defines the scope of the business of insurance in a particular case. Some insight into the actual scope of the phrase can be obtained, however, by distinguishing between cases: that is, the phrase *business of insurance* varies, depending on whether the case involves antitrust or other regulatory matters.

Antitrust cases. In antitrust cases, the courts, especially recently, have interpreted the phrase narrowly, in accordance with the general rule disfavoring expansive interpretations of exemptions to the federal antitrust laws.[3] The current test in antitrust cases lies somewhere between the first two interpretations outlined above. The following three criteria are relevant in determining whether a particular practice is part of the business of insurance exempted from federal antitrust scrutiny:

- *Risk spreading.* The first and most important factor is "whether [a particular] practice has the effect of transferring or spreading a policyholder's risk."[4] This factor reflects the Supreme Court's view

---

[3]See, for example, Union Labor Life Insurance Co. v. Pireno, 458 U.S. 119, 129 (1982). See generally Spencer Kimball and Barbara Heaney, "Emasculation of the McCarran-Ferguson Act: A Study in Judicial Activism," *Utah Law Review*, vol. 1 (1985).

[4]Union Labor Life Insurance Co. v. Pireno, 458 U.S. 119, 129 (1982).

of the core function of insurance, which is to spread risk and not to do other things such as offer investment or management consulting services. Thus, for example, in *Union Labor Life Insurance Co. v. Pireno*,[5] the Court held that a peer review practice for determining reasonableness of chiropractic rates did not constitute the business of insurance, in part because the practice was unconnected with the spreading and underwriting of policyholder risk. Similarly, in *Group Life & Health Insurance Co. v. Royal Drug Co.*,[6] the Court held that agreements between an insurer and participating pharmacies under which the pharmacies supplied prescription drugs to policyholders at cost plus two dollars did not constitute the business of insurance, in part because the agreements did not spread risk but merely passed cost savings on to policyholders and enhanced insurance company profits.

• *Relationship to the insurance policy.* Second, in evaluating whether a particular activity constitutes the business of insurance for purpose of the antitrust exemption, courts look to whether the "practice is an integral part of the policy relationship between the insurer and the insured."[7] The rationale for this factor is that the "relationship between insurer and insured, the type of policy which could be issued, its reliability, interpretation, and enforcement . . . were the core of the 'business of insurance.' "[8] So, for example, in *Union Labor Life Insurance Co. v. Pireno*,[9] the Court held that peer review procedures were not part of the business of insurance, partly because they were not an "integral part of the relationship between insurer and insured."[10]

• *Intra-industry activity.* Third, the courts consider "whether the practice is limited to entities within the insurance industry."[11] This

---

[5]458 U.S. 119 (1982).

[6]440 U.S. 205 (1979).

[7]Union Labor Life Insurance Co. v. Pireno, 458 U.S. 119, 126 (1982).

[8]Group Life & Health Insurance Co. v. Royal Drug Co., 440 U.S. 205, 215–16 (1979).

[9]458 U.S. 119 (1982).

[10]458 U.S. at 131 (1982).

[11]Union Labor Life Insurance Co. v. Pireno, 458 U.S. 119, 129 (1982).

criterion is drawn from the history of the McCarran-Ferguson Act, which, according to the Supreme Court, was largely premised on the "widespread view that it [was] very difficult to underwrite risks in an informed and responsible way without intra-industry cooperation."[12] This factor has contributed to a narrow reading of the "business of insurance" in particular cases. In *Group Life & Health Insurance Co. v. Royal Drug Co.*,[13] for example, the Court held that agreements between an insurance company and participating pharmacies that limited the amounts the pharmacies could charge policyholders for prescription drugs were not part of the business of insurance, in part because the agreements involved "the mass purchase of goods and services from entities outside the insurance industry."[14]

In general, the courts have adopted a sensible approach to defining the business of insurance for antitrust purposes. The three-factor test articulated in the cases, however, suffers from the weakness of all such tests, namely, that it is difficult to determine how the test should come out if the factors point in different directions. Without a weighting of the different factors, it is hard to determine which should trump in the event of conflict. The Court has implied that risk spreading is the most important factor; if that is absent, we would assume that a given practice would not be protected from antitrust scrutiny even if the other factors were present. Beyond this, however, the cases provide little guidance about the relative importance of the three factors.

As a practical and theoretical matter, the current three-factor test appears unnecessarily complicated as a guide to determining the scope of the business of insurance for antitrust purposes. The courts should abandon the needlessly complex factor analysis and substitute the simple rule that, for antitrust purposes, the *business of insurance* means only the process of intra-industry cooperation for the purpose of sharing information and establishing uniform rates and policy forms.[15] These were in fact the practices that the McCarran-Ferguson

---

[12]Ibid., quoting Group Life & Health Insurance Co. v. Royal Drug Co., 440 U.S. 205, 221 (1979).

[13]440 U.S. 205 (1979).

[14]440 U.S. at 224.

[15]For recent decisions in which this type of conduct was found to be central to the

Act was intended to protect. Moreover, our interpretation is consistent with the recent Supreme Court cases, which have emphasized the importance of intra-industry cooperation (the third factor in the current test) and of rates and policy provisions (the second factor) in the process by which risk is passed from policyholder to insurance firm (the first factor).

Thus, we suggest that the courts should apply the following simple, uniform rule in antitrust cases: the *business of insurance* means only the process of intra-industry cooperation for the purpose of sharing information and establishing uniform rates and policy forms.

Other regulatory contexts. So far we have discussed the business of insurance as it applies to the antitrust exemption. It is evident, however, that the interpretation of the phrase for other regulatory purposes is not necessarily the same as for antitrust purposes, for two reasons.

First, the interpretation given the phrase necessarily reflects a balance of competing policy considerations, including the policies deemed to underlie the otherwise applicable federal regulatory scheme. As a functional matter, the courts, in interpreting the *business of insurance,* are adjusting the boundaries between state and federal regulatory programs. The task of statutory construction takes proper account not only of the policies that Congress sought to achieve in the McCarran-Ferguson Act but also of the policies that undergird the potentially applicable federal regulatory scheme. The interpretation given to the *business of insurance,* therefore, is likely to vary depending on the regulatory context in which the case arises.

A leading illustration of this principle is *SEC v. Variable Annuity Life Insurance Co.*[16] At issue in *Variable Annuity* was whether variable annuity contracts offered by insurance companies were within the scope of the business of insurance and therefore exempt from federal regulation under the securities laws. A variable annuity contract— unlike the fixed annuity contract traditionally offered by insurance

---

"business of insurance," see, for example, In re Workers' Compensation Insurance Antitrust Litigation, 867 F.2d 1552 (8th Cir. 1989); Proctor v. State Farm Mutual Automobile Insurance Co., 675 F.2d 308 (D.C. Cir.), cert. denied, 459 U.S. 839 (1982); Owens v. Aetna Life & Casualty Co., 654 F.2d 218, cert. denied, 454 U.S. 1092 (1981).

[16]359 U.S. 65 (1959).

companies—ties the benefits received by the policyholder to the success of the company's investment policy. In other respects, however, the variable annuity resembles traditional fixed annuities in that the company assumes mortality risk: payments are determined based on standard actuarial life expectancy tables, with the insurance company taking the risk that a customer will live longer than expected.

The Supreme Court, through Justice William O. Douglas, concluded that the variable annuity policies were not part of the business of insurance protected by the McCarran-Ferguson Act, because the policyholder bore the investment risk:

> The concept of "insurance" involves some investment risk-taking on the part of the company. The risk of mortality, assumed here, gives these variable annuities an aspect of insurance. Yet it is apparent, not real; superficial, not substantial. In hard reality the issuer of a variable annuity that has no element of a fixed return assumes no true risk in the insurance sense. It is no answer to say that the risk of declining returns in times of depression is the reciprocal of the fixed-dollar annuitant's risk of loss of purchasing power when prices are high and gain of purchasing power when they are low. We deal with a more conventional concept of risk-bearing when we speak of "insurance." For in common understanding "insurance" involves a guarantee that at least some fraction of the benefits will be payable in fixed amounts.[17]

It is easy to fault the reasoning of the *Variable Annuity* case. Justice Douglas asserted that assuming only mortality risk—as the variable annuity policies did—was not "true risk" in the insurance sense. But mortality risk is true risk in every functional sense. Further, the opinion failed to recognize that the standard, fixed annuity also assigns investment risk to the customer: it protects the customer in the event that prices go down, but the customer bears all the risk of price increases.

Despite its analytical shortcomings, the *Variable Annuity* case can be justified, as a matter of policy, on the ground that it represents an adjustment of two statutory schemes; its impact was not to prohibit insurance companies from offering variable annuities but simply to

---

[17]359 U.S. at 71.

subject variable annuities to the regulatory scheme of the federal securities laws. This social policy, more than any abstract reasoning about the nature of "insurance," explains the result in the case.[18]

A second reason why the interpretation of the phrase *business of insurance* is likely to be different in general regulatory contexts from that in the antitrust setting is that the purposes of the McCarran-Ferguson Act were different in the two settings. The act's general exemption for the business of insurance—as opposed to the specific antitrust exemption—was intended to ensure that state regulation and taxation of insurance could continue in the aftermath of the Supreme Court's declaration in *South-Eastern Underwriters* that insurance was commerce. As such, the range of activity protected by the phrase *business of insurance* in the general regulatory context is quite different from the activities protected under the antitrust exemption. The exemption in the general regulatory context protects state regulation and taxation; the antitrust exemption protects intra-industry cooperation for the purpose of sharing information and establishing uniform rates and policy forms.

It is clear, for example, that for purposes of the general regulatory exemption the *business of insurance* encompasses advertising of insurance policies, even though no risk is passed through the advertisement.[19] The term covers a broad range of activities for which an insurance company or agent would need to obtain a license under state law.[20] It covers insurance company activity subject to state safety and soundness regulation and thus would appear to include matters such as capital structure, investment portfolios, policy coverage, and mergers and consolidations.[21] Thus, despite the Supreme

---

[18]For other cases adjusting the boundaries between state insurance regulation and federal securities regulation—and opting for federal law—see SEC v. National Securities, Inc., 393 U.S. 453 (1969)(applying SEC Rule 10b-5 to alleged misrepresentations in shareholder communications incident to proposed merger of insurance firm, even though state insurance authority had affirmed the merger as being fair and not contrary to law); SEC v. United Benefit Life Insurance Co., 387 U.S. 202 (1967)(applying Securities Act of 1933 to annuity contract offered by insurance company).

[19]See FTC v. National Casualty Co., 357 U.S. 560 (1958).

[20]Compare Robertson v. California, 328 U.S. 440 (1946)(applying pre–McCarran-Ferguson Act law).

[21]The cases disagree as to whether the phrase covers priorities of liens against

Court's admonition that the statute "did not purport to make the States supreme in regulating all the activities of insurance *companies*" but only in regulating the "*business* of insurance," the fact is that the regulatory exemption for the business of insurance is considerably broader than the corresponding antitrust exemption.[22]

The Supreme Court has not adopted any generalized test—whether by a factor analysis or otherwise—for determining the scope of the business of insurance in general regulatory cases. As one court recently observed, "We are confronted with a confusing mass of interpretations as to the term 'business of insurance' which leaves basic, fundamental questions unanswered."[23] The Supreme Court, however, has provided some guidance—perhaps, indeed, as much as is possible under the circumstances—by setting forth in the *National Securities* case a "laundry list" of activities that fall within the rubric: "the relationship between insurer and insured, the type of policy which could be issued, its reliability, interpretation, and enforcement," together with "other activities of insurance companies [that] relate . . . closely to their status as reliable insurers."[24] In our view, this approach provides adequate guidance to the meaning of the phrase *business of insurance* outside the antitrust context, and we therefore recommend that it be retained.

---

insolvent insurance companies. Several courts have ruled that state lien priority rules must give way to inconsistent federal rules, notwithstanding the McCarran-Ferguson Act. See Idaho ex rel. Soward v. United States, 858 F.2d 445 (9th Cir. 1988), cert. denied sub nom. Fagiano v. United States, 109 S.Ct. 2063 (1989); Gordon v. United States Department of the Treasury, 668 F.Supp. 483 (D.Md.), aff'd, 846 F.2d 272 (4th Cir. 1987), cert. denied, 109 S.Ct. 390 (1988). These holdings are questionable in light of the fact that insurance company insolvency intimately involves the rights of policyholders under their contracts. Recently, the Sixth Circuit has adopted what we believe to be the better rule that a state liquidation priority scheme for insurance companies was part of the "business of insurance" for McCarran-Ferguson Act purposes. Fabe v. United States Department of the Treasury, 939 F.2d 341 (6th Cir. 1991), cert. granted, 112 S.Ct. 1934 (1992).

[22]SEC v. National Securities, Inc., 393 U.S. 453, 459 (1969)(emphasis added). For a recent case concluding that redlining in insurance is part of the "business of insurance" under the act, see NAACP v. American Family Mutual Insurance Co., 978 F.2d 287 (7th Cir. 1992).

[23]Fabe v. United States Department of the Treasury, 939 F.2d 341 (6th Cir. 1991), cert. granted, 112 S.Ct. 1934 (1992).

[24]SEC v. National Securities, Inc., 393 U.S. 453, 459 (1969).

Scope of State Regulation

Even if a given activity falls within the business of insurance, it does not necessarily follow that federal regulation of that activity will be displaced. Federal law will still apply to the activity in question in three separate situations: (1) if the state has failed to regulate the activity in question in a sufficiently direct or immediate way as to displace federal law; (2) if Congress has explicitly overridden state law in the applicable federal statute; or (3) if the exercise of state regulatory authority is in violation of the federal Constitution. We discuss these situations in turn.

State "Regulation." The McCarran-Ferguson Act does not prevent the federal government from regulating the business of insurance per se. Rather, it bars federal regulation (subject to additional exceptions discussed below) only when the states themselves have exercised their authority over the business. Thus, the antitrust exemption states that the federal antitrust laws apply to the business of insurance "*to the extent that* such business is not *regulated* by State law."[25] The regulatory exemption states that the "regulation or taxation" of the business of insurance is to be left to the states in the absence of clear and specific indication that federal legislation is intended to displace state law, and that, subject to specified exceptions, no federal statute shall be construed to "invalidate, impair or supersede" state laws regulating the business of insurance.[26] If the states have not acted as required by the statute, then federal law applies notwithstanding the McCarran-Ferguson Act.

The issue of whether a state has sufficiently exercised its authority over the business of insurance to obviate federal regulation is present in both the antitrust and the regulatory contexts. The following discussion examines a number of approaches to this issue. As in the case of defining the business of insurance, however, the scope of state activity required to trigger the antitrust exemption may be different from that required to trigger the general regulatory exemption. The statutory language itself suggests a difference between these contexts and a narrower exemption for antitrust than for

---

[25]15 U.S.C. § 1012(b)(emphasis added).

[26]See 15 U.S.C. §§ 1011, 1012(a), 1012(b).

the general regulatory issues: state "regulation" and "taxation" prevail over general federal laws in the absence of specific congressional override; but federal antitrust law is displaced only "to the extent that" the states have not regulated. The limiting phrase *to the extent that* suggests that the cession of power to state regulation is narrower in the antitrust context than in the general regulatory context.

There appear to be four general interpretations of the scope of state regulation necessary to displace federal law. We describe these interpretations in the following paragraphs and proceed to analyze which of these interpretations is most consistent with the goals of the antitrust exemption and the general regulatory exemption.

• Read most narrowly, the reference to state regulation could mean only that if a state *affirmatively mandates* the conduct in question, then the federal laws do not apply.

• Under a second, slightly broader reading of the statute, federal law is canceled only if the state has adopted a regulation *at least as stringent* as that applicable at the federal level. Under this reading, if a state adopts a regulation less stringent than the federal law, then the federal law would not be displaced.

• A third reading, less hospitable to federal enforcement, is that federal law is canceled if a state regulates the insurance industry, even if the regulation is less stringent than that otherwise applicable under federal law, so long as the regulation *concerns the conduct* that allegedly violates federal law and has *objectives broadly consistent* with federal policy.

• Under the broadest interpretation, the state may displace federal regulation by regulating the business of insurance, even if the state's regulation has a purpose *different* from the federal regulation and even if the state regulation is *less stringent* or covers conduct *different from* the otherwise applicable federal law.

The antitrust exemption. In the antitrust context, the cases cluster around the third interpretation above: the federal antitrust laws are displaced if the state law regulates the same conduct as federal antitrust law and serves broadly consistent objectives. Two main types of state legislation might be deemed to displace federal antitrust law: state regulation of substantive conduct and state antitrust laws. We discuss these in turn.

The first type of legislation that might displace federal antitrust

21

law is state regulation of substantive conduct. It is clear that a state may "regulate" the business of insurance so that federal antitrust scrutiny over the regulated activities is precluded, even if the state does not impose any form of antitrust regulation. Thus, private cooperation in determining and setting rates will not be subject to federal antitrust scrutiny, under current law, if a state has affirmatively regulated the rate-setting activity. It is not entirely clear from the recorded cases, however, how much state involvement in rate setting is enough to displace federal antitrust scrutiny. The existing regimes of rate regulation by the states break down into the following broad categories.

• A few states, such as Massachusetts and California (with its required rollback of rates under Proposition 103), affirmatively mandate rates in some lines. Clearly, the antitrust exemption applies to this kind of direct, plenary state regulation.[27]

• A number of states have "prior approval" rules for some or all lines. In a prior approval system, the rates must be filed with the state insurance commissioner and affirmatively approved before use. In general, it would appear that a prior approval requirement would be sufficient "regulation" of rates to displace federal antitrust laws, at least if the approval is a meaningful constraint. The argument that a state prior approval system displaces federal antitrust law is stronger if the state requires that the filed rates must also be within a band of variance from benchmark or target rates issued by the state insurance commissioner. The argument is weaker, however, if approval is shown to be a mere formality or if approval is deemed to have been granted as a matter of law if the state does not act within a given period.

• Many states have adopted "file-and-use" or "use-and-file" laws. These permit insurance companies to charge rates without prior state approval, subject to a requirement that the rates be filed with the state insurance commissioner either before the rates are charged or soon after the policies are offered at the new rates. In all such states, the insurance commissioner retains authority to bar a company from continuing with its filed rates if the commissioner determines that

---

[27]A rule limited to state-mandated rates would also clearly fall within the state action antitrust exemption. See Parker v. Brown, 317 U.S. 341 (1943).

the rates are discriminatory, excessive, or inadequate. The argument for displacement of state antitrust laws here is weaker than for prior approval regimes for the obvious reason that the state regulation is not in the form of a prior restraint. File-and-use laws represent a somewhat more stringent state regulation than use-and-file laws because the state possesses theoretical power under the former to intervene before the company actually starts charging the rate to the public; but the difference may be unimportant if the notice period before use is short. In addition, the argument for displacing federal antitrust law will be stronger to the extent that the state imposes substantive limits on permissible rates by establishing target rates and prohibiting filed rates that fall outside a band of deviation from the target rates.

• Beginning in the 1970s, a substantial number of states moved to regimes of free-market rates. In these states, the company is not subject to any requirement that its rates remain within a band of a target rate or, usually, to any filing requirements. Insurance commissioners in such states, however, typically retain the authority to interdict rates found to be discriminatory, excessive, or inadequate or, in some states, to represent unfair methods of competition.

In general, the courts and the market have assumed that state regulatory involvement under any of the first three categories above is sufficient to make federal antitrust scrutiny over rate-setting practices unnecessary. The fourth category of deregulated rates, however, has proved more problematic. Arguably, if rates are to be set by market forces, without substantial state oversight, then the state no longer "regulates" this part of the business of insurance, so that price fixing by insurance companies within the state would thereafter be subject to control under the federal antitrust laws. Thus, some observers assume that repeal of rating laws automatically subjects state insurance markets to federal antitrust regulation.[28] If, however, the state, in deregulating rates, has failed to indicate an affirmative intent to allow federal antitrust scrutiny—or if the state has affirmatively indicated an intent to leave the McCarran-Ferguson Act bar in place despite the deregulation—the argument for federal intervention is weaker than if the state has affirmatively consented to

---

[28]See, for example, Zack Stamp, "A Modest Proposal: Repeal of State Rating Laws," *Best's Review*, no. 9, vol. 91 (1991), p. 45.

the application of federal antitrust law.

The application of the McCarran-Ferguson Act to state rate deregulation has not been definitively resolved. In one important case, *In re Workers' Compensation Insurance Antitrust Litigation*,[29] a state (Minnesota) had partially deregulated rates by permitting insurers to write policies at "rates that are lower than the rates approved by the commissioner provided the rates are not unfairly discriminatory.[30] The commissioner retained the power to prohibit unfair methods of competition or unfair or deceptive practices. The Eighth Circuit held that the partial rate deregulation had not lifted the McCarran-Ferguson Act bar to federal antitrust scrutiny: although the state had "determined to promote price competition by leaving to the insurers' competitive judgment the setting of workers' compensation insurance rates below the allowable maximum," this policy "did not repeal the Commissioner's supervisory authority over rate setting practices."[31]

The other general type of state legislation that might displace federal antitrust laws, in addition to state rate regulation, is state antitrust laws. The effect of state antitrust regulation has become more important as an increasing number of states abandon the exemptions that insurance companies have traditionally enjoyed from state antitrust scrutiny.[32]

Here the cases appear to be stricter than in the context of state rate regulation. A leading district court case, *United States v. Chicago Title and Trust Co.*, for example, involved a federal antitrust challenge to allegedly anticompetitive interstate acquisitions by a title insurance firm.[33] The court rejected the argument that the state antitrust

---

[29]867 F.2d 1552 (8th Cir. 1989).

[30]See 867 F.2d at 1557.

[31]867 F.2d at 1558. The court went on, however, to find that the plaintiffs had introduced sufficient evidence in the trial court to trigger the boycott exception to the McCarran-Ferguson Act. The parties settled for $50 million in January 1991, a resolution that received widespread notice in the insurance press. See, for example, Colleen Mulcahy, "WC Insurers Settle Antitrust Suit," *National Underwriter*, January 28, 1991, p. 3.

[32]Texas and California have recently repealed the industry's exemptions from state antitrust law, and campaigns to repeal state exemptions have occurred in Massachusetts, Rhode Island, and other states. See Neil McGhee, "Antitrust Law Exemption Challenged in Mass., R.I.," *National Underwriter*, April 1, 1991, p. 23.

[33]242 F.Supp. 56 (N.D. Ill. 1965).

law displaced federal law under the McCarran-Ferguson Act, observing, in part, that the state did not have on the books "a provision *precisely comparable* to [Clayton Act § 7] prescribing acquisition of stock of another corporation. It is not sufficient that a state have legislated on other . . . antitrust matters."[34] The clear implication is that state antitrust regulation must cover the same conduct and be at least as stringent as the federal regulation to trigger the bar of the McCarran-Ferguson Act. Whether the Supreme Court would go this far, if confronted with the issue, is not known.

The regulatory exemption. In the general regulatory area, it appears that a state will be held to have "regulated" the business of insurance to preclude federal regulation, either when the state has adopted effective regulations that are specifically concerned with the subject matter, even if the state's regulations are not as stringent as the federal regulations, or when the state has regulated the business comprehensively enough to occupy the field of insurance regulation, even if the state does not have a specific regulation directed to the matter the federal government is attempting to control. The cases cluster around the fourth and most general interpretation of state regulation set forth above.

In *FTC v. National Casualty Co.*, for example, the Federal Trade Commission (FTC) sought to apply its rules against deceptive advertising to the activities of insurance companies within the boundaries of states that outlawed unfair insurance advertising and authorized enforcement through administrative supervision.[35] The FTC argued that this state legislation did not displace federal authority because it was too vague and general and had not been embodied in "administrative elaboration of these standards and application in individual cases."[36] Therefore, although the states had legislated, they had not "regulated" as required under the McCarran-Ferguson Act. Reading between the lines, one can infer that the FTC's real objection was that these state regulatory schemes were not being vigorously enforced. The Supreme Court found the argument unpersuasive, however, and announced in a conclusory *per curiam* decision that the state legislation was sufficient.

---

[34]242 F.Supp. at 60 (emphasis supplied).

[35]357 U.S. 560 (1958).

[36]357 U.S. at 564.

Lower court cases have read *National Casualty* as establishing a broad scope for the general regulatory exemption. It is not necessary, for example, that the state statute or regulation deal specifically with the practice in question; it is enough that the state "have a general regulatory scheme governing the conduct of the insurance business."[37] If, however, there is no conflict between federal law and state insurance regulation, federal law may apply even if the matter involves the business of insurance.[38]

Although the scope of state regulation is thus quite broad, there are a number of situations in which state regulatory power will not displace competing federal regulation:

• The mere fact that the state has the *power* to regulate will not be sufficient to keep federal control at bay if the state has not chosen to *exercise* that power. Even if the state's decision not to regulate reflects a deliberate state policy to leave a particular area of commerce to free-market forces, the McCarran-Ferguson Act might not prevent the application of federal regulation to the field deliberately abandoned by state authorities.

• While the state regulations need not be as stringent, or as stringently enforced, as the competing federal rules, they cannot be completely *lacking in substance*. The Court noted pointedly in *National Casualty* that the FTC "does not argue that the statutory provisions here under review were mere pretense."[39] The clear implication was that if the state had attempted to displace federal regulation by pretextual legislation, the Court would have looked through the pretense and held the federal law to be applicable.

• The state regulation will not be held to have precluded federal control of activities engaged in by insurance companies in other states. In *FTC v. Travelers Health Association*, for example, the Supreme Court held that the McCarran-Ferguson Act did not prohibit the application of the Federal Trade Commission Act to allegedly false and deceptive statements made in other states by an insurance

---

[37]McIlhenny v. American Title Insurance Company, 418 F.Supp. 364, 369 (E.D. Pa. 1976).

[38]See NAACP v. American Family Mutual Insurance Co., 978 F.2d 287 (7th Cir. 1992) (federal Fair Housing Act prohibiting redlining held applicable to the business of insurance because not inconsistent with applicable state regulation).

[39]357 U.S. at 564.

company, even though the state of the company's domicile purported to prohibit all deceptive acts and practices by a domiciliary company regardless of location.[40]

Federal Override. Even if a state has "regulated" the business of insurance, federal law still applies if Congress has clearly indicated an intent to preserve the federal law notwithstanding the McCarran-Ferguson Act. Several federal laws are expressly preserved as applied to the business of insurance in the McCarran-Ferguson Act itself, including the National Labor Relations Act, the Fair Labor Standards Act, and the Merchant Marine Act.[41]

Aside from these statutes, express federal legislation overriding the McCarran-Ferguson Act exemption is uncommon. Indeed, Congress has sometimes gone beyond what is strictly necessary and restated an insurance exemption in particular federal statutes. Congress provided in the Employment Retirement Income Security Act (ERISA), for example, that "nothing in this [statute] shall be construed to exempt or relieve any person from the law of any State which regulates insurance, banking, or securities."[42] As courts have recognized, the insurance exemption in ERISA is essentially a restatement of the McCarran-Ferguson Act's general regulatory exemption.[43] Thus, even if Congress had not adopted the ERISA provision, the McCarran-Ferguson Act would probably have removed ERISA control over state-regulated insurance activities.

Congress also addressed the issue of insurance regulation in the Comprehensive Environmental Response, Compensation, and Liability Act (CERCLA).[44] CERCLA expressly preempts state insurance laws that restrict the formation of certain risk-retention pools or purchasing groups.[45] Congress further provided, however, that "nothing in this subchapter shall be construed to affect either the tort law

---

[40]362 U.S. 293 (1960).

[41]15 U.S.C. § 1014.

[42]29 U.S.C. § 1144(b)(2)(A).

[43]The ERISA exemption is interpreted *in pari materia* with the McCarran-Ferguson Act. See, for example, Pilot Life Insurance Co. v. Dedeaux, 481 U.S. 41, 48–51 (1987).

[44]42 U.S.C. § 9601 et seq.

[45]42 U.S.C. §§ 9673–75.

or the law governing the interpretation of insurance contracts of any state,"[46] thus generally retaining the McCarran-Ferguson Act exemption outside the narrow context in which the preemption is explicit.

Constitutional Limitations. Even if a federal statute has not preempted state regulation, the federal Constitution may nullify state attempts to control the conduct of insurance companies.

Police power. It is now perfectly clear, although it has not always been, that states enjoy very broad substantive powers to regulate the business of insurance within their borders, subject, however, to constitutional protections for personal liberties. The scope of state regulatory authority in this regard was more or less definitively established even during the heyday of the so-called *Lochner* era of America's constitutional history. During this period, the Court upheld broad state authority over the business of insurance even as it was striking down a variety of other state efforts to regulate business.[47] Insurance has long been treated as a business "affected with a vast public interest."[48] The constitutional authorization for highly rigorous state regulation is, accordingly, beyond serious question, at least under current law.

Protections for individual liberties. Although states clearly have broad police power to regulate the business of insurance, that power is equally clearly circumscribed by other provisions of the Constitution. Thus, to take the most obvious example, a state could not engage in intentional racial discrimination through its insurance regulation, at least not unless the discrimination was supported by a compelling state interest. Nor could a state interpose regulation without giving the regulated party rights to procedural due process as required under the federal Constitution. For the most part, these principles are obvious and have not generated extensive litigation.

Geographic limitations. Far more problematic is the question of

---

[46]42 U.S.C. § 9672(a).

[47]See, for example, German Alliance Insurance Co. v. Lewis, 233 U.S. 389 (1914)(upholding Kansas rate regulation for insurance firms); La Tourette v. McMaster, 248 U.S. 465 (1919)(upholding state regulatory power over insurance brokers).

[48]Prudential Insurance Co. v. Benjamin, 328 U.S. 408, 415–16 (1946).

the geographic extent of state regulatory power. Because the business of insurance is effectively nationwide, one state's effort to regulate that business often creates effects in other states. The problem of interstate effects is present in a variety of industry contexts, but it is particularly acute in the insurance business because the insurance contract itself is intangible. It is often impossible to locate any defined *situs* for the contract rights at issue; the policy itself may have been negotiated across state or international lines and may subsequently be assigned to parties in still other jurisdictions; and the person or property on which the insurance is obtained may suffer harm in a variety of remote locations. In addition, because insurance is highly regulated by the states, states frequently impose their laws on insurance-related activities. These factors have made insurance regulation the single most fertile breeding ground for cases involving principles of legislative jurisdiction—that is, the power of a state under the federal Constitution to apply its law to transactions or relationships that may involve occurrences, parties, or rights located or arising in foreign jurisdictions.

The leading early precedent in this area is *Allgeyer v. Louisiana*.[49] This was an action by the state of Louisiana against a Louisiana firm that had taken out a policy of marine insurance with a New York insurance company on a shipment of cotton to a foreign port. The insurance company had not complied in all with respects with the Louisiana law regulating the marine insurance business. The Supreme Court held that Louisiana could not properly regulate the transaction. The contract had been made in New York, with the only act in Louisiana being the mailing of a letter by the insured to the insurance company in New York. Given these minimal contacts between the state of Louisiana and the transaction, the state's law could not be applied consistently with the due process clause of the Fourteenth Amendment:[50] a citizen of a state, said the Court, has "a

---

[49]165 U.S. 578 (1897).

[50]The case is chiefly remembered today for its eloquent—if subsequently repudiated—list of the activities falling within the realm of protected "liberty" under the due process clause:

> not only the right of the citizen to be free from the mere physical restraint of his person, as by incarceration, but . . . the right of the citizen to be free in the enjoyment of all his faculties; to be free to use them in all lawful ways; to live and work where he will; to earn his livelihood by any

29

right to contract outside of the State for insurance on his property—
a right of which state legislation cannot deprive him."[51] Here the
Court ran into some analytical difficulty, because an analysis based
solely on the right of a citizen to engage in contracts under the due
process clause would seem to invalidate regulation of *intrastate*
transactions as much as *interstate* transactions. Yet the power of a
state to regulate insurance contracts *within* its borders was clear and
indeed had been established in an earlier case.[52] The Court resolved
the problem by *ipse dixit:*

> It may be conceded that [the] right to contract in relation to
> persons or property or to do business within the jurisdiction
> of the State may be regulated and sometimes prohibited when
> the contracts or business conflict with the policy of the State
> as contained in its statutes, yet the power does not and cannot
> extend to prohibiting a citizen from making contracts of the
> nature involved in this case outside of the limits and jurisdic-
> tion of the State, and which are also to be performed outside
> of such jurisdiction.[53]

Allgeyer was extended in later cases to justify relatively expansive limits on state authority to regulate insurance transactions in
other states. In *St. Louis Cotton Compress Company v. Arkansas*, the
Court considered the legality of an Arkansas statute taxing insurance
premiums paid by an out-of-state owner to an out-of-state insurance
company to ensure property located in Arkansas.[54] The Supreme
Court, through Justice Oliver Wendell Holmes, had little difficulty
invalidating the statute on the authority of *Allgeyer* but, significantly,
rested the decision not on broad notions of substantive due process
but rather on the fact that "the Arkansas tax manifests no less plainly
than the Louisiana fine a purpose to discourage insuring in companies
that do not pay tribute to the State."[55] It was the parochial purpose

---

lawful calling; to pursue any livelihood or avocation, and for that purpose
to enter into all contracts which may be proper, necessary and essential
to his carrying out to a successful conclusion the purposes above men-
tioned (165 U.S. at 589).

[51]165 U.S. at 591.

[52]Hooper v. California, 155 U.S. 648 (1895).

[53]Allgeyer v. Louisiana, 165 U.S. at 591.

[54]260 U.S. 346 (1922).

[55]260 U.S. at 349.

of the legislation that caused its invalidation, not some interference with generalized rights under the due process clause. Holmes concluded that "a state may regulate the activities of foreign corporations within the state but it cannot regulate or interfere with what they do outside."[56]

The principle that a state may not regulate insurance transactions occurring outside its borders never applied to situations in which the state asserting regulatory jurisdiction was the domiciliary state for the insurance company. The courts have always recognized that domiciliary states have broad regulatory authority. A classic early case is *Hartford Life Insurance Co. v. Ibs.*[57] The insured had failed to pay an assessment on a mutual life insurance plan, resulting in cancellation of the policy a few days before his death. The beneficiary sued in Minnesota state court for the death benefits, alleging that the assessment in question was illegal since the company had improperly accumulated large excess margins that were available to pay death benefits without assessment. The defendant set up as a defense a prior decree of the Supreme Court of its domiciliary state, Connecticut, which had affirmed the company's right to levy the assessment. The U.S. Supreme Court held that the Connecticut decree was conclusive as to the rights of the policyholder, even though the policyholder had not been party to the action, since the Connecticut courts had jurisdiction over "all questions relating to the internal management of the corporation."[58]

In *Home Insurance Co. v. Dick,* an insured residing in Texas (Dick) sued in Texas courts on a contract of marine fire insurance that had been issued in Mexico by a Mexican company to a resident of Mexico to cover losses in Mexican waters.[59] The defense was that Dick, an assignee of the policy, had failed to bring suit within one year as required by the contract. Dick successfully contended in the state courts that the time-bar provision was ineffective under a Texas statute that purported to invalidate contractual provisions cutting off certain rights of action. The Supreme Court held, however, that the Texas statute could not constitutionally be applied to bar the defense.

---

[56]Ibid.

[57]237 U.S. 662 (1915).

[58]237 U.S. at 671.

[59]281 U.S. 397 (1930).

31

The Court defined the limits of a state's legislative jurisdiction as follows: "A State may . . . prohibit and declare invalid the making of certain contracts within its borders. Ordinarily, it may prohibit performance within its borders, even of contracts validly made elsewhere, if they are required to be performed within the State and their performance would violate its laws."[60] A state, moreover, could prohibit the enjoyment by persons within its borders of rights acquired elsewhere that violate its laws or public policy and in some cases could refuse to aid in the enforcement of such rights.[61] But the state could not apply its laws to invalidate a contract that had no connection with the state other than the fact that it had been assigned to a party residing there.

In *John Hancock Mutual Life Insurance Co. v. Yates,* an insured obtained a policy of life insurance in New York on the basis of material written misrepresentations about his health.[62] After his death, which occurred soon after the policy was issued, his beneficiary moved to Georgia and sued to recover the death benefit in the courts of that state. The company set up the misrepresentation as a defense, but the beneficiary alleged that the insured had truthfully reported his medical condition to the agent, who had not recorded the information in the application. This argument was good under Georgia law but bad under New York law. The Court declared that the Georgia courts were required to respect the New York law under the full faith and credit clause of the Constitution.

A different fact situation was presented in *Pacific Employers Insurance Co. v. Industrial Accident Commission.*[63] Here a Massachusetts employee of a Massachusetts employer was injured while temporarily detailed to a California facility of the employer. The employee sued the employer's California workmen's compensation carrier and invoked the benefits of the California workmen's compensation statute, which were more generous than those available under the Massachusetts statute. The insurance company defended on the ground that the California courts were required to give full faith and credit to the Massachusetts statute. The Supreme Court held that the

---

[60]281 U.S. at 407–08.

[61]281 U.S. at 410.

[62]299 U.S. 178 (1936).

[63]306 U.S. 493 (1939).

California court could properly apply the California statute under the full faith and credit clause, observing that

> in the case of statutes, the extra-state effect of which Congress has not prescribed, as it may under the constitutional provision, we think the conclusion is unavoidable that the Full Faith and Credit Clause does not require one state to substitute for its own statute, applicable to persons and events within it, the conflicting statute of another state, even though that statute is of controlling force in the courts of the state of its enactment with respect to the same persons and events.[64]

Because California had a valid legislative concern with the bodily safety and economic compensation of employees injured within its borders, it was free to apply its own law to the occurrence, even though Massachusetts law would have applied if the events had taken place in that state.[65] The *Pacific Employers Insurance Co.* case established that a state could apply its own law to govern the legal consequences of accidents occurring within the state, even if the accidents involved relationships previously established in other states. More generally, the case seemed to establish that the state in which the key events giving rise to the legal dispute occurred always had legislative jurisdiction to apply its law in litigation in that state's courts.

In the important case of *Allstate Insurance Co. v. Hague,* the Court addressed a claim for insurance benefits brought by a beneficiary in Minnesota court based on an insurance policy that had been delivered in Wisconsin covering an accident in Wisconsin involving only Wisconsin residents.[66] The Minnesota Supreme Court held that Minnesota law governed the case and that under Minnesota law, though not under Wisconsin law, a beneficiary could stack the uninsured motorist coverage clauses on separate automobiles to increase the coverage limits. The court held that Minnesota conflict-of-laws rule required application of Minnesota law, because it was the "better rule."

The U.S. Supreme Court affirmed in a plurality opinion. De-

---

[64]Ibid. at 502.
[65]Ibid. at 503.
[66]449 U.S. 302 (1981).

33

claring that the constitutional analysis was fundamentally the same under the due process clause and the full faith and credit clause[67]— a point that had been in some doubt—the plurality observed that a state's choice of law would be invalidated under the Constitution if the state whose law was being applied "has had no significant contact or significant aggregation of contacts, creating state interests, with the parties and the occurrence or transaction."[68] If, in contrast, the state had sufficient contacts so that "choice of its law is neither arbitrary nor fundamentally unfair," then the state could constitutionally apply its law.[69] On the facts of the case, the plurality found sufficient contacts with Minnesota on the grounds that: (1) the insured was employed in Minnesota; (2) the insurance company was doing business in Minnesota; and (3) the beneficiary became a Minnesota resident before bringing suit, for reasons not having to do with the litigation.

The decision in *Allstate Insurance Co.*, despite its broad language, does not resolve the constitutional questions because it enjoyed the assent of only a plurality of the court. Justice John Paul Stevens concurred only in the judgment, articulating as the relevant constitutional standard the proposition that "the [full faith and credit] Clause should not invalidate a state court's choice of forum law unless that choice threatens the federal interest in national unity by unjustifiably infringing upon the legitimate interests of another State."[70] The three dissenting justices (Lewis Powell, Warren Burger, and William Rehnquist) agreed with the plurality that a state's application of its law should be invalidated "only when there are no significant contacts between the State and the litigation."[71] In their view, however, the contacts with Minnesota were so minimal as to fail even this "modest check on state power."[72]

The Court's most recent foray into this tangled web was a noninsurance case, *Phillips Petroleum Co. v. Shutts*.[73] This was a

---

[67]449 U.S. at 308 and n. 10.

[68]449 U.S. at 308.

[69]449 U.S. at 313.

[70]449 U.S. at 323 (Stevens, J., concurring in the result).

[71]Ibid. (dissenting opinion).

[72]449 U.S. at 332.

[73]472 U.S. 797 (1985).

34

class action by owners of natural gas royalties on leases located in eleven different states, brought in Kansas state court against a purchaser who had allegedly failed to make timely payments for gas taken from the leased lands. The vast majority of the leases (99 percent) and the plaintiffs (97 percent) had no connections with the state of Kansas aside from their participation in the lawsuit.[74] The gas purchaser, however, owned property and conducted a substantial business in Kansas, and several hundred of the 33,000 plaintiffs were Kansas residents. Justice Rehnquist—writing this time for the majority—defined the test as being whether Kansas had a "significant contact or significant aggregation of contacts" with the claims asserted by each member of the plaintiff class, contacts "creating state interests" to ensure that the application of Kansas law was "not arbitrary or unfair."[75] Judged by this standard, Kansas did not have sufficient contacts to apply its law constitutionally to all the claims at issue in the case, especially since the parties to many leases had no reason to believe that Kansas law would control.[76]

This line of cases does not support any clear-cut rule for state legislative jurisdiction over the insurance business. It would appear, however, that the Constitution at least provides states with considerable leeway to regulate insurance transactions with significant interstate contacts. As long as there are sufficient minimum contacts between the state and the transaction in question, the state may constitutionally apply its law, even if other states also possess legislative jurisdiction. Those cases in which the Supreme Court held that state legislative jurisdiction did not exist represent extreme situations in which a state reached out to apply its law to a transaction with only marginal contacts, if that, with the state.

Our conclusion—that the Constitution imposes only minor constraints against extraterritorial application of state insurance regulation—raises the question of why the states do not appear to have engaged in an internecine regulatory war in attempts to apply their law to as wide a range of practices as possible. There appear to be

---

[74]472 U.S. at 815.

[75]472 U.S. at 821–22, quoting Allstate, 449 U.S. at 312–13.

[76]472 U.S. at 822. The Court offered no guidance on which law applied, other than to observe that in many cases the law of more than one state could constitutionally apply. See ibid. at 823.

several reasons for the surprisingly peaceful conditions in state insurance regulation notwithstanding the potential for regulatory conflict that appears built into the constitutional structure.

First, the states have a long history of working together through organizations such as the National Association of Insurance Commissioners (NAIC) to devise regulations that respond to the legitimate regulatory concerns of the different states involved. These organizations have operated as effective checks against the incentive that states might otherwise have to compete to apply their own laws to interstate transactions. Further, the dynamics of federalism play a significant role here: state insurance regulators have always been aware that if they fail to devise workable strategies for interstate accommodation, they will risk losing their regulatory authority altogether because the federal government might be inclined to enter the picture. The pervasive threat of federal preemption has always operated to induce cooperation among state insurance regulators.

Second, the insurance business itself is amenable to a relatively straightforward allocation of jurisdictional responsibilities among state regulators. Principal responsibility for solvency regulation is quite naturally assigned to the state in which a given insurance company has its domicile, subject to the power of other states to bar out-of-state insurers from writing policies in the state if the out-of-state firm is considered to present unacceptable risks to policyholders in the state. Regulation of insurance policies can be roughly, but effectively, allocated on the basis of the location of the insured. Regulation of the relationship between agencies and insurance companies can be committed to the state in which the agency is located. Regulation of advertising and other trade practices can be undertaken by the state in which the advertising or trade practices take place. This allocation is not perfect by any means, and in many situations, especially in the case of commercial lines, it may not unambiguously identify a primary regulator. But for most purposes, these rules of thumb quite effectively determine which state should take the lead in regulating a particular transaction or practice.

Third, the McCarran-Ferguson Act itself, as interpreted by the Supreme Court, has tended to inhibit regulatory conflict among the states. In the leading case of *FTC v. Travelers Health Association*,[77]

---

[77]362 U.S. 293 (1960).

the Court held that the "state regulation which Congress provided should operate to displace . . . federal law means regulation by the State in which the [practice] has its impact."[78] Specifically, the Court held that an insurance company's domiciliary state could not displace federal regulation of practices occurring in other states merely by adopting legislation purporting to regulate the activities of the domiciliary company in other states. Although the *Travelers Health Association* case is not directly concerned with the constitutional constraints on state action, it discouraged vigorous attempts by states to export their laws to conduct occurring elsewhere because it suggested that such state laws would be ineffective to trump otherwise superseding federal regulations.

Although in general the rule-of-thumb allocations of state regulatory authority described above have proved remarkably stable and successful, there are some signs of possible breakdown in state cooperation in the area of antitrust regulation. California's Proposition 103 applied that state's antitrust rules to insurance companies—rules that California officials at least consider to be more stringent than the corresponding federal laws.[79] Moreover, the state's attorney general took the position that "it does not matter where the [conduct creating liability] takes place. You cannot comply with California's antitrust laws by breaking them in another state or country. If the effects are felt in California, California law applies."[80] If Proposition 103 is enforced as strictly as these comments suggest, the result could be to export California's stringent antitrust rules to regulate the conduct of insurance companies all over the country, on the theory that such conduct has "effects" in the California market. It remains to be seen whether the California initiative will disrupt the system of interstate cooperation in insurance company regulation.

Models of State Regulation

So far we have outlined the ways in which the Constitution and federal and state statutes allocate jurisdiction over the insurance industry

---

[78]362 U.S. at 298–99.

[79]See Joanne Wojcik, "California Antitrust Rules Anger Industry," *Business Insurance*, May 21, 1990, p. 3.

[80]Ibid.

between the states and the federal government. We are now in a position to formulate a general theory about the dynamic structure of this system of regulatory federalism. In this section, we contrast three scenarios of the dynamics of insurance regulation within a federal system: the concerted withdrawal model, the race-to-the-bottom model, and the state regulation model. The arguments for and against federal regulation differ depending on which of these models is chosen as best reflecting the realities of contemporary insurance markets.

Concerted Withdrawals. Under one scenario, a deterioration of regulatory standards could occur where insurance companies threaten to leave a state en masse unless the state adopts regulations that help the insurance industry but hurt consumers. Faced with this kind of threat, the states capitulate to the insurance industry's demands on the theory that having some insurance available, even on inadequate terms, is better than having none at all. The result would be regulation that inadequately protects consumers and unjustifiably enriches insurance companies.

There is some evidence that this kind of conduct might have occurred from time to time in the past. The industry's ability to implement this sort of concerted action under present conditions, however, is very limited. If in fact the insurance business in the state is profitable at the time of the threat to leave, the firms that leave will sacrifice these profits as well as their business goodwill by departing. If the business is profitable, moreover, some firms will not leave, knowing that the departure of competitors will leave a rich market for them to exploit. The low barriers to entry in insurance also suggest that start-up firms will quickly be established to pick up the market share that the existing firms have abandoned.

The scenario of an industry threat to leave as a way to extort benefits at the expense of consumers is, accordingly, unrealistic unless the industry itself is highly organized for concerted action with very effective sanctions against firms that refuse to cooperate. This type of organization may once have existed for some lines—particularly fire insurance—but even given the remaining pockets of industry cooperation, there is little evidence that an effective threat of group withdrawal could be organized today, except in unusual market settings, if the purpose were solely to extort consumer benefits rather than to leave a market that had truly become unprofitable.[81]

Race to the Bottom. A second model of regulatory federalism in insurance markets draws on an analogy to corporate law regulation. Under one well-known theory, the competition of states for corporate charters (and the tax revenues and other income that corporate charters provide) stimulates the development of a "race to the bottom" in which states vie with one another to offer the menu of regulations most desired by corporate managers, even though in so doing they permit managers to engage in egregious abuse of shareholder interests.[82] As applied to insurance firms, the argument might be that states will compete to become the domiciles of insurance firms in order to obtain the resulting taxes, jobs, and other benefits; and to attract insurance firms to their borders, they offer a regulatory regime that serves the interests of insurance firms but harms those of policyholders.

Whatever its merits as a description of corporate law, the race-to-the-bottom theory is not particularly convincing as applied to insurance regulation, for a number of reasons.[83]

First, it ignores the effect of policyholder choice in insurance markets. If an insurance firm domiciled in a given state offers a product permitted under the law of that state with features inimical to consumer welfare, that product is not likely to fare well in competition with more desirable products offered by other companies. Constrained by consumer choice, insurance companies are not likely to demand legal regimes that permit them to abuse consumer welfare; and even if such regulatory regimes exist, insurance companies are not likely to take advantage of them.

Second, in the case of policy terms, it is not possible for a firm

---

[81]An agreement to withdraw from a state to extort anticonsumer regulation would already be arguably subject to federal antitrust scrutiny under the boycott exception to the McCarran-Ferguson Act.

[82]The race-to-the-bottom theory is most prominently associated with William Cary; see Cary, "Federalism and Corporate Law: Reflections upon Delaware," *Yale Law Journal*, vol. 83 (1974), p. 663. The notion of a competition in laxity, however, has been prevalent in American corporate law theory since the early part of the century.

[83]For our own contribution to this debate, see Jonathan R. Macey and Geoffrey P. Miller, "Toward an Interest-Group Theory of Delaware Corporate Law," *Texas Law Review*, vol. 65 (1987), p. 469.

to export costs to policyholders located in other states as it is possible, for example, for a corporation chartered in one state to export the costs of promanagement rules onto shareholders located in other states. As described above, regulation of policy terms is mostly under the control of the state in which the insurance customer is located. Thus, even if a firm's state of domicile allowed its insurance firms to engage in egregious or abusive practices toward policyholders, the state in which the policyholder is located is not likely to do so.

Third, exportation of costs is theoretically possible in the case of insurer solvency regulation, as opposed to regulation of policy rates and provisions. But insurance companies do not have a strong incentive to induce their states of domicile to issue excessively lax solvency regulations. The larger, established insurance companies, which hold political power in a given state, are likely to prefer, on the contrary, quite stringent solvency regulation. Stringent solvency regulation can impede entry of new competition; for example, if substantial capital is required to open a new insurance company in the state, fewer new companies will be formed. Further, the established firms in the industry are likely to prefer relatively stringent capital regulation to bolster the reputation of their domiciliary state as a reliable regulator of solvency. Such a reputation for the regulator redounds to the benefit of firms in the state by providing credible signals of their own solvency and good business repute. It is true that some state might attempt to attract insurance company charters by offering lenient solvency regulation, but the consequence would be to draw the worst-capitalized and most failure-prone firms, while potentially driving well-capitalized firms domiciled in the state to seek incorporation elsewhere to preserve their reputations. Further, other states would have the right to bar firms chartered in the low-regulation state from writing policies within their borders if such firms were deemed to present excessive insolvency risks.

Fourth, because of the geographic configuration of insurance markets described above, each state regulates the most important features of insurance transactions occurring in the state. One practical impact of this multistate regulation is that it is likely to remove any inducement that large firms might have to move to states with lenient, anticonsumer regulations. To realize economies of scale, large firms need to use the same forms, policies, and procedures in all states in which they operate. Therefore, if one state is particularly stringent, the large firms are likely to adjust their entire business operations to comply with the requirements applying in that state alone. There tends to be a one-way ratchet for large firms in the direction of complying with more stringent regulations. But it is exactly the large firms that, in the race-to-the-bottom theory, are likely to move their domiciles to take advantage of lenient legal regimes. Smaller firms are not likely to do so because the transactions costs of moving exceed whatever benefits they could obtain from doing so. Accordingly, the large insurance firms are not likely to demand particularly lenient legislation or to respond to state inducements to change domiciles to obtain such favorable treatment.

Fifth, in the case of insurance regulation, unlike general corporate regulation, there exists an elaborate mechanism for cooperation and communication among the state regulatory bodies. The practical necessity that state insurance solvency regulators face of working together provides powerful disincentives to any given state to initiate a competition in laxity. Such antisocial behavior would likely be met by retaliation from other state regulators, which could impose significant costs on any state regulator who sought to poach on other states' domains.

For all these reasons, the regulatory pattern in the insurance industry does not appear structured in a way that induces a competition in laxity. Not surprisingly, there appears to be very little movement of insurance firms away from their states of domicile, and firms—even the very largest firms—have usually remained in the states in which they were initially chartered. Moreover, there is no convincing evidence that the states in which the largest insurance companies are domiciled—New York, New Jersey, Illinois, Connecticut, Massachusetts, California, and others—have engaged in any sort of competition in laxity; on the contrary, these states appear to be among the more stringent insurance regulators nationwide.

State Regulation. Our analysis of the first two models suggests that in the absence of other state intervention—such as rate regulation—competitive insurance markets will be characterized by free entry and exit and will not be plagued by any systematic tendency to favor the interests of the insurance industry over those of policyholders. We now consider the impact of state rate regulation.

41

State regulation of rates—either by direct administrative control or by deference to industry rating bureaus—poses the danger of systematic bias, either in the direction of rates that are too high (that is, above market-clearing rates) or too low (below market-clearing rates).

Consider first the scenario in which rates are set too high. It is not necessary to posit that the state insurance commission is "captured" by the insurance industry for this situation to occur. All that is required is that the commission sets rates that tend to differ from market-clearing rates. If the rate set initially by the commission is below the point of reasonable profit, insurance firms will begin to withdraw coverage in the state.[84] These withdrawals would not be part of any conspiracy to elicit regulatory favors but would simply reflect the fact that the less efficient firms cannot operate at a profit under the applicable regulations. The withdrawals, in turn, induce protests by policyholders and, eventually, provide a reason for the insurance commission to raise rates back to market-clearing levels (or above).

If, in contrast, the rate initially set is too high, the natural corrective effect of withdrawals will not be present. No firms will leave the market. There are, to be sure, several natural checks to excessively high rates. Insurance firms are likely to engage in nonprice competition, thus dissipating some of the excess profits; and eventually high prices are likely to induce consumer complaints. In general, however, the dynamics of the market would appear to result in rates above market-clearing levels in situations where rates are set administratively.

Different considerations apply if we posit the existence of aggressive, well-organized consumer interests in the state. These groups may be able to obtain rate rollbacks and even reductions of rates below market-clearing levels. The natural response of the less efficient firms in the industry would then be to withdraw from the state to avoid continued losses. Thus, if firms can withdraw without incurring additional losses, the impact of consumer groups is likely to be temporary: firms in the state's market may find some of their

---

[84]Withdrawals continue today; a prominent example is the decision by seven large companies to leave the Massachusetts automobile insurance market to escape that state's rate-setting system. See Henry Stimpson, "Massachusetts Mirage?" *Insurance Review*, vol. 50 (1989), p. 36.

wealth expropriated, but in the long run the effect of withdrawals will be to drive rates back up to or beyond market-clearing levels. Recent experience in several states, however, suggests a possible additional factor: if a state can impose a sufficiently high "exit fee" or tax on firms wishing to withdraw from the state, then the withdrawal option may not be feasible even for a firm operating below its cost, if the present value of the losses associated with the tax exceed the present value of the losses associated with continued operation in the state. Recent proconsumer statutes—such as California's Proposition 103 and the omnibus Texas statute—have included exit restrictions of various sorts.[85] If a state can effectively neutralize the withdrawal threat, it may be able to expropriate the wealth of shareholders— especially shareholders of out-of-state firms—for the benefit of policyholders in the state.[86]

---

[85]The Texas legislation, for example, requires insurers to file a withdrawal plan and obtain approval from the insurance commissioner before leaving the market, bars a firm from reentering the state for five years after withdrawal from the market, unless the commissioner approves an earlier reentry, and requires a substantial notice period before termination of agency agreements. See Jaelene Fayhee, "Texas Reforms Pass by Big Margin," *National Underwriter*, June 3, 1991. The California law did not prohibit automobile insurers from exiting the market entirely but did severely restrict the power of firms selectively to exit the market by canceling policies. See Cal. Ins. Code § 1861(c); Calfarm Insurance Co. v. Deukmejian, 48 Cal. 3d 805, 771 P.2d 1247, 258 Cal. Rptr. 161 (1989).

[86]One recent study documents significant negative stock price effects surrounding the time of the adoption of Proposition 103. See Roger M. Shelor and Mark L. Cross, "Insurance Firm Market Response to California Proposition 103 and the Effects of Firm Size," *Journal of Risk and Insurance*, vol. 57 (1990), p. 682. When the data were disaggregated to distinguish between insurers with heavy California involvement and non-California insurers, however, the study found no significant impact for the in-state firms and large, statistically significant negative responses for the out-of-state firms. The authors of this study postulate that the effect reflects differences in firm size, but an equally plausible explanation is that firms with heavy involvement in California are able to exercise political influence to receive relatively more favorable regulatory treatment than firms with only a small California presence.

The inference that Proposition 103 and similar programs might be used as instruments for in-state favoritism is reinforced by actual events. In California, for example, the current insurance commissioner has declared that income from investments outside of California will be included in the California rate base, thus subjecting out-of-state firms to the possibility of multiple counting on their out-of-state investment income. See Joanne Wojcik, "New Regulator Freezes Rates under Prop. 103," *Business Insurance*, January 14, 1991, p. 1. In New Jersey, a measure adopted in March 1990 required automobile insurers to assume $1.4 billion of the

We believe that the state regulation model presents the most accurate picture of the dynamics of regulatory federalism in the insurance industry. It predicts that, aside from the matter of rates, the regulatory system is unlikely to display any systematic favoritism for insurers and against policyholders as a result either of systematic withdrawals or of interstate competition for charters. It predicts, further, that the business of insurance is likely to be conducted in an economically efficient manner in states without rate regulation. In states *with* rate regulation, however, the model predicts that rates will either equal or exceed market-clearing levels in most cases. In states where two factors coalesce, however—active, organized, and enduring consumer political groups and significant exit fees on withdrawals—the result may well be the opposite, namely, sustained below-market rates.

A Preliminary View of Federal Regulation. We now apply these results to draw some tentative conclusions about the utility of federal insurance regulation. Later parts of this volume will address questions of federal regulation in a number of specific settings.

The analysis presented so far strongly suggests that federal regulation is not generally needed as a corrective to systematic anticonsumer bias in the existing structure of insurance regulation, with the possible exception of rate regulation. Finally, our analysis suggests, however, that administrative rate setting is likely to result in systematically skewed results—either too high or, where consumer groups are powerful and exit fees are imposed, too low. This finding suggests that federal preemption might be useful to remove the unnecessary overlay of state rate regulation and to ensure that rates are set by market forces.

---

debt of the state's Joint Underwriting Association; see Ruth Gastel, *Rate Regulation,* Insurance Information Institute, July 1991; the result was to expropriate the wealth of company shareholders located all across the country for the benefit of a class of New Jersey motorists.

3

The Antitrust Exemption

WE NOW ADDRESS the McCarran-Ferguson Act's antitrust exemption. It should be observed at the outset that the McCarran-Ferguson Act provides no harbor against scrutiny under *state* antitrust laws. Historically, many states have exempted the business of insurance from their own antitrust laws as well, so that the practical effect of the McCarran-Ferguson Act was to protect the industry from antitrust scrutiny of any sort. In recent years, however, states have begun to apply their own antitrust laws with greater vigor. Some states, including, most recently, Texas, have repealed the industry's exemption from state antitrust regulation. As of year-end 1990, the insurance industry was, for practical purposes, subject to full antitrust scrutiny under state law in twenty-eight states.[1] Although merely being subject to a state's antitrust law did not necessarily mean that an insurance firm would be scrutinized as vigorously as it would if federal law applied, it is evident that state regulators are increasingly favoring the use of their own antitrust laws to control anticompetitive behavior by insurance firms.[2]

The McCarran-Ferguson Act provides a partial exemption from federal antitrust law and in so doing stands in some tension with basic principles of competition that structure the vast majority of economic activities in the United States. As the Supreme Court has observed, the national policy favoring free competition and disfavoring cartels is "pervasive," "fundamental," and "essential to economic

---

[1] See Edward J. Muhl, "A Ceasefire in the War of Words," *Best's Review*, vol. 91, no. 8 (1990), p. 28.

[2] One political effect of this increased use of state antitrust laws may be to mitigate the industry's traditional opposition to McCarran-Ferguson Act reform, on the theory that many of the benefits of the act are already lost if the industry is subject to vigorous antitrust scrutiny under state law.

freedom."[3] Against the background of such a fundamental policy, any exemption from the federal rules against private collusion in the setting of price must overcome a substantial burden of persuasion.

After examining the various rationales advanced to support the federal antitrust exemption, this chapter looks at the scope of the exemption as applied by the courts. It then addresses the probable impact of applying federal antitrust scrutiny to the industry.

Rationales for the Exemption

First, we consider the arguments typically advanced in favor of the antitrust exemption.

Information Sharing and Efficiency. The most cogent argument for the antitrust exemption is that it facilitates the economically efficient sharing of information to evaluate risk and to price insurance accurately.[4] According to this argument, the activities of industry rating bureaus are intended to serve the socially efficient goal of accurate pricing and are not designed to facilitate any sort of anticompetitive price fixing. Even if private rating bureaus do have a small anticompetitive effect, so the argument goes, the social costs of the reduction in competition are more than outweighed by the social efficiencies that such bureaus make possible.

The argument starts with the observation that faulty pricing of insurance products causes harmful economic distortions and inefficiencies. If rates are set too low, the effect will be to subsidize risky activities by insureds, resulting in social costs of excessive activity levels imposing social harm. Excessively low rates, moreover, will cause insurance firms to be unprofitable, resulting in the departure of some firms from the industry and the underprovision of insurance by those that remain. Shortages will occur, and some parties will find themselves unable to obtain insurance at all.

If rates are set too high, insurance firms will prosper, but policyholders will pay too much; socially desirable activities will be

---

[3]Federal Trade Commission v. Ticor Title Insurance Company, 60 U.S.L.W. 4515, 4518 (June 12, 1992).

[4]See Daniel J. McNamara, "Toward a New Environment: History of Rating Bureaus and Insurance Regulation," *Best's Review*, vol. 91, no. 2 (1990), p. 53.

discouraged. Some customers will be unable to afford insurance at all and will be forced either to abandon their activities, such as driving or owning a home, or to self-insure in a situation where an insurance contract could have been obtained if the product had been priced correctly. And the high rates will reduce the incentive to operate efficiently that insurance firms would face in an unregulated pricing environment; waste and inefficiency in the provision of insurance services will result.

Cooperation among insurance companies is necessary to achieve accurate pricing in the industry—at least for casualty and property lines. Insurance premiums reflect the provider's evaluation of the probable costs of paying claims, as well as other costs of doing business, and a reasonable provision for profit. But in the case of property and casualty lines, the cost of claims payable in the future is difficult to assess at the time the policy is written, because the probability of an event occurring and the severity of the event if it does occur are both difficult to calculate. Proper evaluation of risk requires extensive sampling of past occurrences of the events insured against, as well as analysis of the historical sample, to predict losses in the future.

This sampling and analysis can be accomplished only by cooperative efforts among insurers. Cooperation serves two principal purposes. First, it makes historical loss data available in a sufficiently large sample to provide a high degree of statistical reliability in the analysis. In the absence of cooperation, each firm might hold its own historical loss data as a form of proprietary information, and it would be difficult for any insurance firms except the largest companies to base their loss predictions on a reliable sample of past experience.[5] Second, cooperation achieves economies of scale because the sampling and analysis need only be done once, by an industrywide rating bureau, rather than many times within individual firms. For both these reasons, under this argument, cooperative rating bureaus are necessary to achieve accurate insurance pricing, at least in the property and casualty insurance business.

The strength of the economic argument for information sharing

---

[5]See Francis Achampong, "The McCarran-Ferguson Act and the Limited Insurance Antitrust Exemption: An Indefensible Aberration?" *Seton Hall Legislative Journal*, vol. 15 (1991), pp. 141–69.

depends substantially on the types of information being shared. Historically, rating bureaus have provided three general types of information to firms in the industry: *historical loss costs; prospective loss costs; and profit margins, operating expenses, and advisory rates.* We discuss these in turn.

Historical loss costs. The argument for sharing information within the industry is persuasive as applied to historical loss data for property and casualty insurers.[6] It is true that property and casualty firms might obtain broadly based historical loss data even if they were barred from directly sharing data with competitors. An independent consulting firm, not in the insurance business, could purchase historical loss data from many firms, compile the data, and then sell them back to assist firms in their pricing decisions. The transactions costs associated with such a third-party arrangement may be high, however, and firms may not have confidence in the data or analysis provided by the consulting company. They may also be unsure that the data provided to the consulting company by their competitors are fully accurate. Problems such as these may make information-sharing arrangements within the industry itself the most efficient means of gathering and compiling historical loss data for property and casualty lines.

Prospective loss costs. The economic justification for sharing historical loss data extends to the analysis of data once compiled although the argument here is somewhat less compelling. Insurance rating bureaus offer not just historical cost data but also prospective analysis that projects future costs. Although the details of prospective analysis may differ across rating bureaus, there appear to be two key elements in most systems, *loss development analysis* and *trend analysis.*[7]

A rating bureau may attempt to take account of the fact that payments are often not made for years or even decades after the

---

[6]The argument is somewhat less plausible for life and health insurance firms, since mortality and morbidity statistics are available from a variety of public and private sources outside the insurance industry.

[7]As we discuss below, there are two principal nationwide rating bureaus in the property and casualty area: the Insurance Services Office, Inc., which serves most property and casualty lines, and the National Council on Compensation Insurance, which serves workers' compensation lines.

policies in question have expired. *Loss development analysis* measures changes in historical incurred losses resulting from late reported claims and changes in dollar values for claims already reported.[8] Loss development analysis uses new information to project future costs of claims on past policies. The argument for sharing information about future policy losses for claims on past policies is quite strong. Such information sharing avoids duplication of effort and would not easily occur in the absence of collaborative activity because much of the data on which the loss development analysis is based is proprietary information in the control of individual companies.

While loss development analysis is used to estimate what the ultimate losses will be for claims associated with past policies, *trend analysis* addresses the losses associated with *future* policies.[9] Trend analysis takes account of significant economic or legal changes likely to affect losses on future policies, including the inflation rate, changes in the law, and increases or decreases in the frequency of claims. The effect of these changes is to make historical, developed loss costs an unreliable measure of losses on future policies. Trending is designed to correct for these distortions.

While the argument for collaborative efforts in loss development analysis is strong, the argument is somewhat weaker for trend analysis. There is no problem of proprietary information for many aspects of trend analysis; provided that the raw data are available, anyone can analyze them. The inflation rate, for example, is readily available from a wide range of sources, and economic science has yet to develop a reliable technique for estimating the rate of future inflation.[10] The argument for trend analysis is considerably stronger with respect to categories of data, such as developments in claim frequency or judgment amounts, that remain the property of individual companies if not shared in collaborative activities.

Although conducting trend analysis through a rating association avoids duplication of effort, this kind of data analysis is not an exact

---

[8]Insurance Services Office, Inc., "Using the Past to Predict the Future: Historical Data, Loss Development and Trend," vol. 7 (1989).

[9]See ibid.

[10]There are enormous arbitrage profits to be made if one could accurately predict future inflation rates; the fact that we do not observe such profits being made on a systematic basis indicates that no one in the market has any reliable method for "beating" the market with respect to future inflation.

science. The presence or absence of a trend is often a matter of judgment, as is the evaluation of whether a given trend will wax, wane, or remain constant. Industrywide reliance on the trend analysis of a rate-making bureau might actually be inefficient because if the projection proved inaccurate, the result would be massive mispricing, whereas if many firms performed their own analyses, the combined contribution of the different assessments might produce a more informed market price. Moreover, smaller firms would not be precluded from obtaining trend information in the absence of an industrywide rating bureau; presumably consulting firms would be ready and willing to conduct these analyses and sell the results to numerous companies.

Trend analysis may also include projected administrative costs of claims resolution. These include the costs of processing claims as well as anticipated litigation costs from claims not resolved at the administrative level. Predictions of rating bureaus about future costs of claims processing and litigation have little economic rationale. Each individual firm is best equipped to predict its own expenses, which vary across firms because of a multitude of unique factors. Calculating administrative and litigation expenses together in a broad-based average, developing the information to account for predicted future expenses, and supplying the analysis back to the industry might provide little information of real value.

Under these circumstances, it appears that cooperative efforts at trending analysis should probably be permitted, from an efficiency standpoint, although the legal system should be diligent to ensure that trending is not used as an aid to the establishment of standardized rates among competing firms.

Advisory rates. Rating bureaus have traditionally incorporated all their data analyses into final advisory rates.[11] These advisory rates are based on the bureau's analysis of historical loss costs,

[11]It should be noted, in this regard, that the major industry rating associations are making giant strides toward limiting the types of information they supply to firms to reduce the potentially anticompetitive effects. As discussed further below, both the ISO and the NCCI are moving away from advisory rates and toward a focus on historical loss data. The ultimate effect of these changes may be to move the industry in the direction of free competition over rates. See Kevin Thompson, "McCarran-Ferguson Repeal and the ISO's Advisory Rate Ban: A Chance for Compromise?" *Northern Kentucky Law Review*, vol. 17 (1990), p. 373.

developed loss costs, and trend but include a loading for expenses of operation and profit as well:

- *Expenses of operation.* We see no justification for general expense information being provided by a centralized industry rating bureau. A rating bureau is unlikely to be in any better position to predict future costs of operation than an individual insurance company. Costs of operation vary across firms for many different reasons: overhead, marketing, employee compensation, and many other costs vary widely from firm to firm. There is no reason to believe that any particular figure for such expenses is optimal. Because each firm is the best judge of its future expenses, rating bureaus provide little information of economic value when they derive average expense figures to be used in the process of setting advisory rates.

- *Standard profit margin.* Nor, in our view, is there any economic justification for a rating bureau's use of a standardized provision for profit in the derivation of advisory rates. The traditional profit margin used by rating bureaus in the property and casualty field was set in 1921 at 5 percent of premiums. This 5 percent profit figure was not based on any analysis of data. It did not even reflect actual profits, since a substantial proportion of the profits of any insurance firm comes from investment income rather than premiums. The continued use of any sort of standardized profit figure for the industry, based on percentages of premiums or otherwise, is unwarranted.

- *Fully developed advisory rates.* Finally, there is no justification, in our view, for the promulgation of final advisory rates as a means of facilitating efficient premium pricing. Advisory rates provide no real information to firms beyond what the firms could provide for themselves on the basis of historical and prospective loss analysis— other than information about prices the firm is expected to charge and what prices other firms will charge. There is no basis for supposing that firms are unable to set their own rates, once they have the necessary loss information, nor is there any plausible argument that rate setting by an industry bureau avoids an inefficient duplication of efforts by the individual firms. Firms in every competitive industry set their own prices; yet we do not imagine that the research and analysis that go into these pricing decisions represent some sort of inefficient duplication of effort that should be avoided by reference to a single pricing bureau. Insurance is no different. Advisory rates serve little function other than discouraging competition. [12]

Thus, our analysis suggests that economic argument in favor of the use of pooled information for purposes of setting prices depends on the nature of the information at issue. The argument is persuasive with respect to historical loss data and developed loss costs; weaker, but still persuasive, with respect to trend analysis; and unpersuasive as applied to final advisory rates.

The fact that sharing of data within the industry is economically efficient in limited circumstances, however, does not necessarily translate into an argument for retaining the McCarran-Ferguson Act's antitrust exemption. As will be seen below (in this chapter), existing doctrine under federal antitrust law would allow firms in the industry to share data freely, without fear of antitrust liability, in many cases where such data sharing is economically desirable. Nevertheless, we will argue that on balance, the case for repealing the McCarran-Ferguson Act is not yet established, provided that existing law polices against cooperative activities in the industry that pose serious threats to competition.

Standardizing Policy Forms. A second argument in favor of the antitrust exemption is that it allows the use of standard policy forms, which have traditionally been issued by the industry's rating bureaus. [13]

Standard policy forms serve several social policies. They facilitate comparison shopping by consumers. With a standard form in

---

[12]Advisory rates may have even more pernicious effects. For an argument that the widespread use of advisory rates contributes to insurance crises such as that which occurred in the 1980s, see Jay Angoff, "Insurance against Competition: How the McCarran-Ferguson Act Raises Prices and Profits in the Property-Casualty Insurance Industry," *Yale Journal on Regulation*, vol. 5 (1988), pp. 397–415. For a different, and more plausible, explanation, see George Priest, "The Current Insurance Crisis and Modern Tort Law," *Yale Law Journal*, vol. 96 (1987), p. 1521, arguing that the crisis in liability insurance was due to judicial compulsion of increasing levels of third-party insurance for victims.

[13]The actual degree of standardization imposed by the rating bureaus is a matter of some debate. It seems clear that policies are least standardized in commercial lines, where the size of the policy and the uniqueness of the risks involved often result in individual negotiation of important policy terms. Personal lines such as homeowners, automobile, and health insurance are more standardized.

place, a consumer need only shop around on the basis of price. If forms were not standardized, in contrast, the consumer would have a difficult time comparing policies because the lower price of one policy might be more than offset by the reduced coverage offered by that policy. Without standardized forms, consumers would have to wade through the fine print of each policy to assess the effective costs of the various deductibles, exclusions, and exemptions. This is time-consuming for the consumer; but more important, the consumer lacks a methodology for determining the actual economic value of particular items of coverage, since that value can be determined only through the sorts of actuarial analyses that are now conducted by firms and rating bureaus. In the absence of effective comparison shopping, the industry is likely to be both less efficient and less competitive than it is already.

A second important economic advantage of standardized forms is that they facilitate the compilation of data necessary for the analysis of risk categories and severity. In the absence of form standardization, it would be difficult to compile an adequate statistical data base on which to assess risks.

Third, language in standardized forms becomes highly precise over time as a result of judicial and administrative interpretations. Court decisions interpreting contract terms, for example, have important impacts throughout the industry if policy provisions are standardized. Other things being equal, it is desirable that the terms of the policy be as precise and determinate as possible, to reduce the incidence of coverage disputes and to facilitate the efficient transfer of the desired amount of risk from insured to insurer. The need for clear terms is particularly compelling in the insurance industry because of the danger of opportunistic behavior in contract interpretation by both the insured and the insurer at the time a claim is made.

These are significant advantages. In our view, the advantages are sufficiently great as to justify a wide range of cooperative behavior within the industry intended to develop and refine standardized forms.

The advantages of standardized forms, however, do not necessarily justify the establishment of industrywide uniform policies that *exclude* the use of forms or policies *other* than the standardized models. First, it should be noted that the advantages of uniform policies in facilitating comparison shopping may be overstated. While it is true that uniform policies make comparison shopping easier, they do not provide consumers with assurances that they are getting equal value with each policy, especially in property and casualty lines. Uniform policy terms do not mean that insurers will pay out on claims with equal promptness or that they will admit coverage in the same cases when claims arise. Insurance companies can differ markedly in their willingness to pay out claims, and the mere standardization of policy forms provides the consumer with no information about these *post hoc* behaviors. Further, some insurance companies are better capitalized than others, and standardized forms provide consumers with no information about the default risk associated with otherwise similar policies.

Second, the advantages of uniform policy provisions at encouraging comparison shopping, facilitating data collection, and enhancing the certainty of interpretation must be assessed against the cost of such provisions in reducing flexibility. Under a system of rigidly controlled uniform forms, a customer and an insurance company would be unable to negotiate a contract that would be in each of their interests if it could be enforced. It is doubtful that such extreme rigidity in policy terms occurs frequently in practice; a sufficiently motivated customer can probably obtain substantial variations from the usual terms. But standardized policies do introduce stickiness into the process by which policies are negotiated, and to this extent they may impair the ability of the contracting parties to arrive at optimal arrangements.

Third, standardized policies could well develop, even in the absence of centralized, industry-affiliated direction, simply as a result of market forces. Consumers might demand standardized policies, especially for personal lines, even if no industry bureaus were in place to issue such forms. The industry could move toward the use of standard forms even in the absence of centralized direction, just as other industries have achieved substantial standardization without resort to potentially anticompetitive industrywide bureaus.

On balance, the argument that a centralized industry association should be allowed to write standardized policies to achieve the benefits of easy price comparison and certainty of application has force. The standard forms should be only suggested, however, and not exclude either the standard forms proposed by others, firm-specific forms, or individually negotiated forms. Any activities on the part of the rating bureau or others to coerce the use of standardized forms goes beyond the economic justification.[14] The ultimate decision about which forms prevail in the industry can and should be left to market forces.[15]

Avoiding Unnecessary Litigation. Opponents of current efforts to repeal the antitrust exemption argue that subjecting the insurance industry to federal antitrust scrutiny will represent a bonanza for plaintiffs' lawyers, who will descend on the insurance industry like a swarm of locusts in search of rich treble damages and attorneys' fees awards.[16] The suggestion is that the principal effect of applying the federal antitrust laws to the insurance industry will be to enrich lawyers at the expense of everyone else.

This argument appears overinclusive as a justification for the McCarran-Ferguson Act. *All* private antitrust litigation, regardless of the industry involved, is conducted by trial lawyers, many of them motivated more by the wish for hefty attorneys' fees than by altruistic concern for consumer welfare. But Congress has made the judgment that across a wide range of industries the benefits of private antitrust

---

[14]The Supreme Court is now considering an important case in which the scope of the boycott exemption as it relates to standardized forms is at issue. In re Insurance Antitrust Litigation, 938 F.2d 919 (9th Cir. 1991), court granted sub. nom. Hartford Fire Insurance Co. v. California (113 S.Ct. 52 (1992). It should be noted that the allegations in the complaint are disputed by the defendants.

[15]For a defense of the activities at issue in the case, see George Priest, "The Antitrust Suits and the Public Understanding of Insurance," *Tulane Law Review*, vol. 63 (1989), p. 999, arguing that the coverage withdrawals were designed to enhance insurance availability to low-risk insureds by segregating them into separate pools from high-risk insureds. It is not clear, however, why patterns of boycott and coercion, if they occurred as alleged, were necessary to accomplish the desirable policy objective of segregating risks into actuarially accurate groups. Ian Ayres and Peter Siegleman respond to Priest by questioning his assumption that insurers cannot differentiate between high- and low-risk consumers but that consumers themselves can (and thus the low-risk consumers can decide to self-insure). Ayres and Siegleman argue that the insurer-defendants in these cases were involved in exclusionary instead of "collusionary" anticompetitive behavior, attempting to exclude smaller firms from the market and thus reduce competition. See Ian Ayres and Peter Siegleman, "The Economics of the Insurance Antitrust Suits: Towards an Exclusionary Theory," *Tulane Law Review*, vol. 63 (1989), p. 971.

[16]See statement of S. Roy Woodall, Jr., in H.R. 9 Hearings.

enforcement—in compensating those who have suffered from anti-competitive pricing practices and in deterring such socially inefficient behavior in others—outweigh the costs, including the costs of litigation. It is not clear why the insurance industry should be different from other industries subject to private enforcement with treble damages and attorneys' fees awards. [17]

Preserving Smaller Firms. Another argument in favor of the antitrust exemption is that, without it, smaller firms in the insurance industry "may be forced to go out of business entirely or be absorbed by larger companies." [18] If insurance firms are not allowed to share information, the smaller firms may suffer disproportionately. Only the larger firms will be able to assess future losses accurately because their own operations will give them access to a large data set of historical costs and because the expenses of analysis can be spread over their large policyholder base. Thus, in the absence of information sharing, the insurance industry will be forced to restructure, with costly and disruptive departures of smaller firms from the market. The end result, according to this argument, would be an industry concentrated in a few large and potentially oligopolistic firms.

Repeal of the antitrust exemption would probably harm some smaller firms. But the principal "harm" from applying the antitrust laws to the industry would not be to smaller firms per se but to inefficiently managed firms that cannot compete when prices are set at competitive, market-clearing levels. Most of these inefficient firms may be among the smaller firms in the industry—not only because smaller firms are likely to be less efficiently managed in some cases but also because most firms in the industry are small relative to the ten or twenty largest firms. But many small firms are likely to do well and even prosper under a regime of truly competitive pricing. Economies of scale in the insurance industry, while they exist, are not nearly as pronounced as in many other industries. [19] Some states,

---

[17]To the extent that private enforcement does pose special problems for the insurance industry, it could be restricted by statute; for example, private plaintiffs could be limited to compensatory damages only.

[18]See Achampong, "The McCarran-Ferguson Act and the Limited Insurance Antitrust Exemption," p. 141; and statement of S. Roy Woodall, Jr., in H.R. 9 Hearings.

[19]See, for example, Christopher Dauer, "Size No Object in Insurer Expenses,"

such as Illinois, have operated with competitive pricing for many years now, with no major shakeout among the smaller firms. The testimony from the banking industry suggests that a smaller firm can do very well, even in head-to-head competition with industry giants, if it is well managed and maintains good customer relations.[20]

Moreover, there is no valid economic reason to maintain small firms in operation simply because they are small, if they are inefficiently managed. Propping up badly managed or inefficiently organized firms harms consumers by subsidizing inefficient producers at the expense of efficient ones, rewards poor performance rather than good performance, and reduces the efficiency of the insurance function within the economy as a whole. A regulatory regime in which insurance firms were not allowed to fail would be undersirable as a matter of public policy.[21] Application of the antitrust laws to the insurance industry would no doubt increase the incidence of insurance company failures at the margin, but failure is the inevitable result of a price system that offers great benefits to consumers of insurance products and to the economy as a whole.

Maintaining Federal-State Balance. Another argument—or, rather, a congeries of related arguments—in favor of the antitrust exemption draws on ideals of federalism. The states, it is said, should continue to police the competitive practices of insurance companies within their jurisdictions in the interest of preserving the appropriate

---

National Underwriter, October 29, 1990, reporting a study showing that "the size of an insurance company is not a major determinant of efficiency"; Neil A. Doherty, "The Measurement of Output and Economies of Scale in Property-Liability Insurance, *Journal of Risk and Insurance*, vol. 48 (1981), p. 57; Randall Geehan, "Returns to Scale in the Life Insurance Industry," *Bell Journal of Economics and Management Science*, vol. 8 (1977), p. 497, (finding only weak evidence of statistically significant returns to scale in the Canadian life insurance industry).

[20]Many smaller banks in upstate New York were able to beat branches of the big New York City banks in direct competition when that state allowed statewide branching. See, for example, Kathleen King, "Upstate New York: Tough Market for City Banks," *Economic Review of the Federal Reserve Bank of Atlanta*, vol. 30 (1985). The banking analogy is not exact, however, because even the smallest banks could offer accounts backed by federal deposit insurance, something that smaller insurance firms cannot do.

[21]See Dale Taussig, "The Case for Bank Failure," *Journal of Law and Economics*, vol. 10 (1967), p. 129.

balance of power between state and federal authority. Repeal of the antitrust exemption would impose "unwarranted federal scrutiny" on an industry already regulated by the states.[22] It would deprive policyholders of regulatory protections at the level closest to them— the states.[23] And it would add an extra layer of regulation, resulting in a costly and uneconomical dual regulatory system.[24]

As applied to the antitrust exemption, this argument is misconceived. The limited federal overlay represented by the antitrust laws is no more intrusive on state powers than is the application of federal antitrust laws to any other business subject to state oversight and supervision. If federal antitrust regulation "steals the fire" of state antitrust regulation to some degree, this should not be a matter of grave concern to the states, since both state and federal antitrust laws are designed to accomplish the same general policy objective of ensuring free and competitive markets.

Preserving Competition. Finally, some have argued that, far from being anticompetitive, the antitrust exemption is in fact *procompetitive* and that repeal of the act would reduce competition and would harm the interest of consumers. The principal argument here is based on numbers. Proponents of the exemption observe, quite correctly, that the insurance industry is anything but monolithic. There are large numbers of providers in the marketplace—by one account, nearly 6,000 life, health, and property and casualty companies and 400,000 agents.[25] And the numbers have been increasing: for example, there were 1,895 U.S. life insurance firms in 1979 and 2,350 in 1989.[26] Insurance, moreover, is extraordinarily unconcentrated in virtually all lines and markets; in the property and casualty line, for example, "no single firm has more than 10% of the national market, and the 10 largest companies account for less than 40 percent of the premium volume."[27]

---

[22]Statement of S. Roy Woodall, Jr., in H.R. 9 Hearings.

[23]Ibid.

[24]Ibid.

[25]Ibid.

[26]American Council of Life Insurance, *1990 Life Insurance Fact Book* (Washington, D.C., 1990), p. 103.

[27]Insurance Information Institute, *1990 Property/Casualty Insurance Facts*, p. 10.

Given this dramatic lack of concentration, the proponents of the antitrust exemption argue, the industry is obviously highly competitive.[28] On the one hand, federal antitrust scrutiny is not needed to enhance competition; on the other hand, federal scrutiny would actually reduce competition in the industry, because the inevitable effect would be to drive many of the smaller to mid-sized firms from the market, thus concentrating the industry and facilitating anticompetitive behavior.

This argument is not well taken. The fact that the industry is unconcentrated does not necessarily establish that it is highly competitive. Above-market pricing can still occur in an unconcentrated industry if there is either a highly effective cartel in operation or if prices are set above market-clearing levels by government fiat. In the banking industry, for example, the nation's 12,000 or so commercial banks operated, until fairly recently, under governmentally mandated price controls, which limited the amounts banks could pay in interest to depositors and prohibited the payment of any interest at all in the case of checking accounts. These price controls, combined with other regulations, permitted many smaller banks to survive and therefore contributed to a highly unconcentrated industry. But it would strain credibility to suggest that the banking industry was fully competitive at the time: it could not have been fully competitive since banks were prohibited from competing on the basis of price in their most important market.

Similarly, in the insurance industry, the price of contracts with policyholders has traditionally been regulated both by the actions of private cartels and by government controls. The pervasive presence of these price regulations—some of which remain in effect today in one form or another—suggests that the large number of insurance companies, and especially the many smaller providers on the market, might reflect not so much vigorous competition as government price protection.

It may well be that application of federal antitrust scrutiny to the insurance industry will lower profit margins in the industry and drive some firms out of business. But as we have already noted, the loss of these firms due to competitive forces would represent a social

---

[28]See, for example, Franklin W. Nutter, "The Flawed Consumer Agenda," *Best's Review*, vol. 91, no. 11, p. 28; Muhl, "A Ceasefire in the War of Words," p. 28.

benefit, since almost by definition the firms forced to leave the industry or merge with other providers would be the less efficient ones. The industry itself is so highly unconcentrated that even the departure of large numbers of firms from the market would not cause significant concerns about competition, except perhaps in a few specialized markets.

The Boycott Exception

The antitrust exemption does not apply to "any agreement to boycott, coerce, or intimidate, or act of boycott, coercion, or intimidation."[29] The interpretation of this exception is vitally important, since if the boycott exception is construed broadly, the antitrust exemption loses much of its power to protect anticompetitive activities within the industry.

Possible Interpretations. As in the case of other key phrases in the McCarran-Ferguson Act, the boycott exception is susceptible to a variety of interpretations yielding important differences in outcomes:

• Read most narrowly, the exception could apply only to the principal abuse against which it appears to have been directed: the refusal by insurance companies to deal with independent agents or other insurance firms that engaged in rebating or other practices that firms within the industry wished to deter.[30]

• A broader reading would include any concerted activities directed at competitors or customers that have the purpose and effect of completely denying them the benefit of competition in "vital matters such as claims policy and quality of service."[31]

• A still broader interpretation would bar concerted activities by insurance firms that have the purpose and effect of limiting access by customers, agents, or competitors to the benefits of competition in

---

[29]15 U.S.C. § 1013(b).

[30]This is the major abuse complained of in the legislative history. See, for example, 91 Cong. Rec. 1485 (1945)(remarks of Sen. O'Mahoney).

[31]St. Paul Fire & Marine Insurance Co. v. Barry, 438 U.S. 531, 553 (1978). For an analysis that advocates roughly this reading, see Joseph E. Coughlin, "Losing McCarran Act Protection through 'Boycott, Coercion, or Intimidation,' " *Antitrust Law Journal*, vol. 54 (1985), p. 1281.

any aspect of the insurance business, even if they do not foreclose a market altogether. This interpretation would allow firms to use cooperative rating bureaus to establish rates but would deny them the power to enforce rates once they had been established.

It might seem plausible to assume that the third interpretation is obviously preferable since it provides maximum protections for competition while remaining within the reasonable limits of the statutory language. This third interpretation, however, stands in some tension with the background and purposes of the McCarran-Ferguson Act. The act was clearly intended to permit the continued operation of state rating bureaus in some form (perhaps under state regulation). But a bureau that establishes and enforces uniform rates effectively amounts to a group boycott within the meaning of this third interpretation. If all the firms in the industry agree to charge only a certain rate, and not less, the effect is to deny customers the benefit of competition with respect to the rates they can obtain on insurance policies. Yet such concerted activity cannot be a group boycott within the McCarran-Ferguson Act unless the boycott exception were to swallow up the entire antitrust exemption.

Judicial Decisions. The Supreme Court wrestled with these issues in the leading case of *St. Paul Fire and Marine Insurance Co. v. Barry*.[32] This case involved an alleged conspiracy by medical malpractice insurers to refuse to deal with policyholders in a company that altered its coverage from an "occurrence" basis to a "claims made" basis. The purpose of the alleged conspiracy was to prevent policyholders from switching insurers in response to the policy change. The defendant insurers argued, among other things, that the boycott exception did not apply to refusals to deal directed at customers rather than competitors. The Supreme Court rejected this argument, holding that the exception "is not limited to concerted activity against insurance companies or agents or, more generally, against competitors of members of the boycotting group."[33] The alleged practices under review amounted to a "boycott" under the statute because they "erected a barrier between St. Paul's customers

---

[32]438 U.S. 531 (1978).

[33]438 U.S. at 552.

and any alternative source of the desired coverage, effectively foreclosing all possibility of competition anywhere in the relevant market. "[34]

The *Barry* decision seemed to endorse the second construction of the boycott exception set forth above, since it emphasized the fact that all possibility of competition in the relevant market had been foreclosed. The case left a great deal unresolved, however, because the presence or absence of a boycott under *Barry* appeared to turn on quantitative factors of how much the concerted activity in question interfered with competitive forces. Activities such as those found to have occurred in *Barry*, which completely foreclosed all possibility of competition anywhere in the market, were within the boycott exception, but the application of the exception to activities that interfered with competition only partially, not completely, remained unclear.

Two recent court of appeals decisions demonstrate that the boycott exception may not be limited to activities that totally foreclose a relevant market and accordingly indicate that the exception may be a major limitation on the scope of the industry's antitrust immunity. *In re Workers Compensation Antitrust Litigation* involved a claim by employers that a state workers' compensation rating bureau had conspired with insurance firms to fix rates for workers' compensation policies in the state.[35] The complaint alleged that the defendants had agreed to boycott other insurance companies and purchasers of workers' compensation insurance to enforce the fixed prices.[36] The district court granted summary judgment to the defendants, but the Eighth Circuit Court of Appeals reversed. The court agreed that mere price fixing—refusals to deal at other than the specified price—would not trigger the boycott exception. But it found that the plantiffs had offered a "plethora of. . . evidence" tending to show that the defendants had agreed to exclude insurers from the rating bureau unless they used the prescribed rates.[37] If proved, this finding was sufficient, in the court's view, to establish the boycott exception and subject the challenged practices to federal antitrust scrutiny.

---

[34]438 U.S. at 553.

[35]867 F.2d 1552 (8th Cir. 1989).

[36]867 F.2d at 1554.

[37]867 F.2d at 1566.

In the second recent case, *In re Insurance Antitrust Litigation*, California and other states challenged certain activities by major insurers and reinsurers in the commercial general liability (CGL) insurance business.[38] The states claimed that the defendants had engaged in a pattern of coercion in an attempt to force the Insurance Service Office (ISO)—an organization of insurance firms that issues standard contracts for the property and casualty industry—to modify its standard CGL insurance form.[39] The complaint alleged that the defendants had refused to deal with the old CGL form, thus effectively forcing the entire industry to adopt the coverages favored by the defendants. The consequence, according to the complaint, was that certain forms of CGL coverage became entirely unavailable.

The district court dismissed the complaints on the ground that they were barred by the antitrust exemption. The Court of Appeals for the Ninth Circuit, however, reversed.[40] It held that the allegations in the complaint sufficiently charged a boycott since, among other things, some of the defendants had allegedly encouraged underwriters in the reinsurance market to refuse to deal with the old form and that the reinsurers had subsequently pressured the ISO to drop the offending form and to adopt one favored by the defendants. The appeals panel interpreted the *Barry* case as not requiring an absolute foreclosure of a market but simply the application of economic pressure for anticompetitive purposes: "The evil of a boycott is not its absolute character but the use of the economic power of a third party to force the boycott victim to agree to the boycott beneficiary's terms." The Supreme Court has agreed to review the decision and may issue a decision clarifying the scope of the boycott exception when it decides the case.

These two recent cases have broadly interpreted the boycott exception by permitting cooperative price-fixing activities but remov-

---

[38]938 F.2d 919 (9th Cir. 1991), cert, granted sub nom. Hartford Fire Insurance Co. v. California, 113 S.Ct. 52 (1992).

[39]Among other things, the defendants allegedly sought the elimination of an "occurrence" clause in the contract and its replacement by a "claims made" provision, which would have eliminated the insurance companies' exposure for claims made after the expiration of a policy. The defendants also allegedly sought to exclude from the standard form contract certain environmental risks, such as accidental pollution.

[40]938 F.2d 919 (9th Cir. 1991).

ing all practical devices, short of state action, for enforcing an agreement once reached. So interpreted, the boycott exception holds the promise of drastically limiting the efficacy of private price-fixing schemes. The standard economic theory of cartels teaches that in a market with numerous firms, no above-market price will long survive in the absence of effective mechanisms for preventing discounts to customers.[41] Thus, if the boycott exception is interpreted and effectively enforced to bar the application of pressure to comply with established rates, the likely effect will be to undermine the efficacy of private rate-setting activities in the first place.

Protected Activities under Federal Law

We now consider three important exemptions from the federal antitrust laws that would remain in effect even if the special exemption for the insurance industry were repealed: the state action doctrine, the rules permitting cooperative sharing of information, and the *Noerr-Pennington* exemption for cooperative lobbying activities.

State Action. The most important exemption for insurance industry rate setting that would survive the repeal of the antitrust exemption is the "state action" immunity of *Parker v. Brown*.[42] Based on "principles of federalism and state sovereignty,"[43] the state action doctrine applies when, first, the challenged restraint on competition is "clearly articulated and affirmatively expressed as state policy" and, second, the policy in question is "actively supervised" by the state itself.[44] The first prong of this test is satisfied even if the state does not directly require the conduct in question, so long as it has evinced an "intent to establish an anticompetitive regulatory pro-

---

[41]For a particularly elegant treatment, see George J. Stigler, *The Theory of Price*, 3d ed. (New York: Macmillan, 1966).

[42]317 U.S. 341 (1943). For a thorough discussion adopting a favorable stance toward state action immunity, see Merrick Garland, "Antitrust and State Action: Economic Efficiency and the Political Process," *Yale Law Journal*, vol. 96 (1986), p. 486.

[43]324 Liquor Corp. v. Duffy, 479 U.S. 335, 343 (1987).

[44]California Retail Liquor Dealers Association v. Midcal Aluminium, 445 U.S. 97 (1980); Accord, Southern Motor Carriers Rate Conference, Inc. v. United States, 471 U.S. 48 (1985).

gram."[45] The second prong is satisfied if "state officials have and exercise power to review particular anticompetitive acts of private parties and disapprove those that fail to accord with state policy."[46]

The extent of state involvement in rate setting necessary to trigger the *Parker v. Brown* immunity is not clear—for the obvious reason that the McCarran-Ferguson Act itself has prevented the litigation of test cases to establish the boundaries of the doctrine in the insurance context. Informed assessments can be made, however, of the likely impact of the state action doctrine if the statute is eventually repealed. Two important recent cases provide substantial guidance on the rules likely to be applied if the industry is placed under the existing scheme of federal antitrust regulation.

In *Federal Trade Commission v. Ticor Title Insurance Company*, the Federal Trade Commission challenged the activities of title insurance companies in allegedly setting rates for title insurance and examination in several states.[47] The rates had been set by private rating bureaus, but the state insurance commissioners possessed the power to investigate the reasonableness of the rates and to veto them if unreasonable. The insurance commissioners, however, had conducted only minimal investigation and had allowed filed rates to go into effect with what appeared to be merely token consideration. The Court of Appeals for the Third Circuit nevertheless held that the collective rate setting was protected by the state action doctrine in all the states.[48] The court held that the states had adopted a clearly articulated and affirmatively expressed policy to displace market rates, emphasizing that the state commissioners had approved the filing of collective rates, that the state statutes recognized the existence of private rating bureaus, and that a federal court should defer to the reasonable interpretations of state law by state administrative bodies. The court held further that the states had engaged in

---

[45]Southern Motor Carriers Rate Conference, Inc. v. United States, 471 U.S. 48, 64 (1985). Thus, where an administrative agency is legislatively required to establish "just and reasonable" rates for an industry, the state action exemption protects collective rate making by firms as permitted by the agency. See also Town of Haille v. City of Eau Claire, 471 U.S. 34 (1985).

[46]Patrick v. Burget, 486 U.S. 94, 101 (1988).

[47]60 U.S.L.W. 4515 (June 12, 1992).

[48]922 F.2d 1122 (3d Cir. 1991). Because it held that the challenged activities were protected by state action immunity, the court did not address the defendants' argument that their actions were protected by the McCarran-Ferguson Act.

the requisite active supervision of collective rate making because they had "demonstrated some basic level of activity directed toward seeing that the private actors carried out the state's policy and not simply their own policy."[49]

The Supreme Court reversed in an important decision limiting the scope of state action antitrust immunity. Holding that "actual state involvement, not deference to private price fixing arrangements under the general auspices of state law, is the precondition for immunity from federal law," the Court determined that the level of state supervision over the rates in question had failed to meet the minimum threshold for state action immunity.[50] In language with broad application to state file-and-use rate systems, the Court stated that

> where prices or rates are set as an initial matter by private parties, subject only to a veto if the state chooses to exercise it, the party claiming the immunity must show that state officials have undertaken the necessary steps to determine the specifics of the price-fixing or ratesetting scheme. The mere potential for state supervision is not an adequate substitute for a decision by the state.[51]

Ticor suggests that the courts will not be willing to read the state action exemption extraordinarily broadly in the rate-setting area. Nevertheless, a substantial range of private activity in the rate-setting area would probably qualify for state action immunity even after the *Ticor* decision. As long as the state insurance regulators actually review the filed rates for substance as well as for form and

---

[49]922 F.2d at 1139.

[50]60 U.S.L.W. at 4518.

[51]60 U.S.L.W. at 4519. The Supreme Court implicitly disapproved the holding of another important recent case, New England Motor Rate Bureau v. FTC, 908 F.2d 1064 (1st Cir. 1990). That case arguably went even further than the court of appeals in Federal Trade Commission v. Ticor Title Insurance Company by way of approving a broad state action immunity in the rate-setting context. At issue was a state administrative system for reviewing rates filed by motor carriers. The court held that the state action exemption applied even though under the state system filed rates became binding unless disapproved and the state had not rejected any rates in recent history or conducted any hearings or investigations. The Supreme Court in Ticor expressed serious misgivings about the analysis in New England Motor Rate Bureau, 60 U.S.L.W. at 4519.

insist on real as opposed to fictional compliance with requirements for disclosure of information underlying the rates and justification of the filed rates based on the information provided, the collaborative activities of private parties in rate setting, subject to administrative review and potential disapproval, should remain within the ambit of *Parker v. Brown* protection. As applied to insurance rate setting, we draw the following inferences from the *Ticor* decision:

• Clearly, the state action doctrine applies when the state affirmatively sets rates, as happens today in a few states. When the rate setting is actually conducted by the state itself, the existence of state action is unmistakable.

• State action is probably also present when a state requires insurers to engage in collaborative rate setting, through rating bureaus or otherwise, and requires that the firms adhere to the rates so established. A requirement of cooperative action constitutes a clearly expressed state policy in favor of such activity, while the mandatory nature of such a system satisfies the second prong of the state action test, at least if the state engages in meaningful scrutiny of insurance companies to ensure their compliance with the state's commands.

• Where the state does not affirmatively require collaborative rate setting, but nevertheless permits it to occur, the cases suggest the following: (1) any statute that expressly authorizes rate setting by rating bureaus or other collaborative mechanisms will be sufficient to protect the cooperative activity under the state action doctrine if the state actively and meaningfully supervises the rate-setting activities to ensure compliance with the legislative goals; (2) even if a statute does not affirmatively authorize collaborative rate setting, the state action doctrine will probably still apply if the insurance commissioner is empowered to establish rates and, pursuant to that authorization, allows collaborative rate setting under active and meaningful administrative supervision as an aid to determining rates; and (3) state action immunity will probably not be present if the state insurance commissioner does not actively and meaningfully supervise the rates or the activities of the private rating bureaus to ensure their compliance, on a case-by-case basis, with the commands of the applicable legislation or regulation.

• State action immunity would probably not apply in states that operate under free-market rate-setting regimes, even if the insurance commissioner permits collective rate-setting activities and retains the power to act against rates deemed discriminatory, excessive, or inadequate. Such schemes would appear to reflect neither a clearly expressed state policy to displace market forces nor an active state supervision of private rating activities.

If, as some have recommended, the antitrust exemption is eventually repealed, the insurance industry is likely to react by seeking revision of state insurance codes to provide state action immunity to a wide range of private rate-setting activities, while at the same time ensuring that the industry participants enjoy the maximum discretion, consistent with the immunity, to set their own rates free of stringent state supervision or control. We view this as a potentially realistic scenario. The Supreme Court's decision in *Ticor*, however, restricts the ability of private insurance companies to organize cartels without meaningful state supervision, and the actions of insurance commissioners would presumably be subject to some degree of political control to the extent that they actively cooperated with a private cartel to fix rates to the detriment of insurance consumers. Accordingly, the Supreme Court's current approach to state action, which significantly prunes back the expansive interpretations offered by a number of courts of appeals, is sufficiently well defined and administrable to obviate the need for special legislation defining the scope of state action in the insurance context.[52]

Cooperative Research. As we have seen, one of the principal justifications for the antitrust exemption is the bona fide need of insurance companies to share information regarding risks and to cooperate in the development of standarized forms. The possibility that federal antitrust laws would prohibit or seriously impede these

---

[52]Francis Achampong argues that the state action doctrine would be an insufficient protection for the insurance industry in the absence of an antitrust exemption because the close supervision requirement would require discarding open competition for flex rating or prior approval systems. See Francis Achampong, "The McCarran-Ferguson Act and the Limited Insurance Antitrust Exemption: An Indefensible Aberration?" *Seton Hall Legislative Journal*, vol. 15 (1991), p. 141. Achampong's major concern is that in the absence of an antitrust exemption, insurance companies will not be able to share loss data, an issue that we address at notes 53–67 and accompanying text.

cooperative activities would be a good reason for retaining at least some of the protections from federal antitrust scrutiny. As currently administered and enforced, however, the federal antitrust laws may not seriously impair the ability of insurance firms to engage in a considerable amount of bona fide sharing of information or cooperative research in the identification and quantification of risks.

The federal antitrust laws have, for many years, been administered with sensitivity to the legitimate needs of industry participants to share certain types of information.[53] As the Department of Justice observed in a 1977 study, *The Pricing and Marketing of Insurance*, existing antitrust law does not prevent competing businesses from undertaking joint activities in which there are economies of scale and which cannot realistically be undertaken by competitors acting alone, so long as the activities in question do not unnecessarily harm competition.[54] This report suggested that the compilation of historical loss costs might well survive antitrust scrutiny if conducted cooperatively, although projection of future prices would raise serious questions. It recommended that such predictive information and analysis be performed by independent consulting organizations rather than by industry rating bureaus.

In 1980, the Justice Department again emphasized the permissibility, under federal antitrust law, of research projects conducted through trade associations or industry joint ventures.[55] Joint ventures of this type are evaluated under a rule of reason and are upheld against antitrust attack if they have a legitimate business purpose, do not hamper competition, and promise benefits to the public.[56] As a

---

[53]See, generally, MacAvoy, ed., *Federal-State Regulation of the Pricing and Marketing of Insurance*, pp. 52–55, concluding that "the antitrust laws clearly permit the joint performance of certain functions, including the formulation of a classification system and statistical plan, and the collection, compilation, and dissemination of past loss and expense data. On the other hand, the projection of future rates, or any large component thereof, would likely fall within the prohibitions of the Sherman Act."

[54]*Report of the U.S. Department of Justice to the Task Group on Antitrust Immunities: The Pricing and Marketing of Insurance* (Washington, D.C.: GPO, 1977).

[55]See U.S. Department of Justice, *Antitrust Guide concerning Research Joint Ventures* (Washington, D.C.: Department of Justice, 1980).

[56]Compare Broadcast Music, Inc. v. Columbia Broadcasting System, 441 U.S. 1 (1979) (joint activities that reduce costs and facilitate efficient marketing of products will be upheld under antitrust laws).

practical matter, joint research ventures are rarely challenged under the Sherman Act,[57] especially if, as in the case of insurance, the industry involved is not highly concentrated.[58]

Congress recognized the need to protect bona fide cooperative research from antitrust scrutiny in the National Cooperative Research Act of 1984.[59] This statute may not strictly apply to the sharing of actuarial information among insurance firms, but it provides insight into the view that Congress has taken on a closely related subject. The statute provides that, in any action under the federal antitrust laws,

> the conduct of any person in making or performing a contract to carry out a joint research and development venture shall not be deemed illegal per se; such conduct shall be judged on the basis of its reasonableness, taking into account all relevant factors affecting competition, including, but not limited to, effects on competition in properly defined, relevant research and development markets.[60]

"Joint research and development venture" is defined as including, among other things, the following activities: "theoretical analysis, experimentation, or systematic study of phenomena or observable facts"; "the extension of investigative findings or theory of a scientific or technical nature into practical application for experimental and demonstration purposes"; and "the collection, exchange, and analysis of research information."[61] In addition, the term *joint research and development venture* specifically includes the establishment and operation of facilities for the conduct of research and the conducting of such a venture on a protected and proprietary basis.[62] The term does not include exchanges of information among competitors that

---

[57]See American Bar Association Antitrust Section, *Antitrust Law Developments*, 2d ed. (Chicago, 1984), p. 52.

[58]See United States v. Container Corporation of America, 393 U.S. 333, 337 (1969). See generally Herbert Hovenkamp, *Economics and Federal Antitrust Law* (St. Paul, Minn.: West Publishing Co., 1985), pp. 110–24.

[59]Pub. L. 98–462, 98 Stat. 1815 (1984), codified at 15 U.S.C. § 4301–4305.

[60]15 U.S.C. § 4302.

[61]15 U.S.C. § 4301(a)(6).

[62]Ibid.

are not "reasonably required to conduct the research and development that is the purpose of such venture,"[63] or conduct or agreements that go to production or marketing as opposed to research and development (other than agreements relating to the proprietary research information itself).[64] Also excluded are agreements related to inventions or developments not created through a research and development venture, or unreasonably regulating participation by a party in other research and development activities.[65] In addition to providing that joint research and development activities be reviewed on a rule-of-reason standard, the act limits the damages available in private antitrust actions based on such activities[66] and permits awards of attorneys' fees to prevailing defendants if a claim is found to be frivolous, unreasonable, without foundation, or in bad faith.[67]

The National Cooperative Research Act does not provide an exemption from all antitrust scrutiny for cooperative research but rather subjects such behavior to a rule-of-reason analysis. This statute, therefore, would not operate as a complete safe harbor for bona fide sharing of information. Nevertheless, its practical effect would be to provide a substantial degree of protection against antitrust scrutiny. Once the analysis is phrased in terms of a rule of reason, as opposed to a per se rule, all the justifications for a given activity are admissible into evidence.

Given the clear-cut antitrust policy argument in favor of sharing certain types of information among competitors, it is unlikely that a bona fide information-pooling venture for historical loss costs in the insurance industry would be subject to a successful antitrust challenge. Similarly, existing antitrust law might not reach legitimately procompetitive information-sharing activities such as the development of prospective lost costs; the preparation, dissemination, and filing of policy forms and classifications; participation in joint underwriting or pools for residual risks; sharing of information relating to fraudulent claims; or certain types of shared research and inspections for purpose of risk classification. This analysis suggests that even the

---

[63]15 U.S.C. § 4301(b)(1).

[64]15 U.S.C. § 4301(b)(2).

[65]15 U.S.C. § 4301(b)(3).

[66]15 U.S.C. § 4303.

[67]Ibid.

repeal of the antitrust exemption would not necessarily bar the types of cooperative activities that economic theory suggests should be undertaken. The question, however, is sufficiently uncertain as to suggest the utility of retaining the existing antitrust exemption, provided that it is interpreted to permit vigorous antitrust enforcement against cooperative activities that harm or threaten to harm the competitive process.

Lobbying. A third possible exemption for industry activity that would survive the repeal of the antitrust exemption is the *Noerr-Pennington* protection for joint political activities.[68] The argument would be that cooperative activities by insurance firms for the purpose of sharing information or even developing proposed rates are nothing other than a form of petitioning state regulators in an attempt to influence state policy and, accordingly, are protected by the *Noerr-Pennington* rule. If the antitrust exemption were repealed, the *Noerr-Pennington* doctrine would offer an obvious potential bulwark to protect collective rate-making activities.[69]

It is unlikely, however, that the *Noerr-Pennington* doctrine will be extended so far as to immunize private activity that fixes prices or otherwise restrains competition, even if the ostensible purpose is to influence government action. The leading precedent is the Fifth Circuit's decision in *United States v. Southern Motor Carriers Rate Conference.*[70] The court held that the *Noerr-Pennington* doctrine did not immunize rate-setting activities by private motor carrier rate bureaus, even when the purpose of the activities was to develop joint rates to be filed with state regulatory bodies. The court distinguished

---

[68]See Eastern Railroad Presidents Conference v. Noerr Motor Freight, Inc., 365 U.S. 127 (1961); United Mine Workers v. Pennington, 381 U.S. 657 (1965); California Motor Transport Co. v. Trucking Unlimited, 404 U.S. 508 (1972).

[69]The U.S. Supreme Court has ducked this argument once, although not in an insurance context. See Southern Motor Carriers Rate Conference, 471 U.S. 48, 55 n.17 (1985). For an analysis concluding that the Noerr-Pennington doctrine protects a substantial range of collective conduct by the insurance industry, see Robert W. Hammesfahr, "Antitrust Exemptions Applicable to the Business of Insurance Other than the McCarran-Ferguson Act: The State Action Exemption and the Noerr-Pennington Doctrine," *Antitrust Law Journal*, vol. 54 (1985), p. 1321.

[70]672 F.2d 469 (5th Cir. 1982), aff'd en banc, 702 F.2d 532 (1983), reversed on other grounds, 471 U.S. 48 (1985).

between the rate-setting activities, which were not protected under
Noerr-Pennington, and the actual activity of presenting rates to the
state commissions or of seeking regulatory permission to engage in
joint activities, which was protected:

> While the joint efforts of the bureaus to secure legislation or
> commission regulation permitting collective ratemaking pro-
> cedures would clearly fall within the ambit of the *Noerr*
> protection, inasmuch as it would seek to influence policy,
> collective action to determine the rates which the bureaus
> desire the commission to approve is not of the same genre.[71]

The State Antitrust Alternative

State antitrust laws represent an alternative regulatory system that, if
effective, might obviate the need for federal oversight. We believe,
however, that state antitrust laws do not represent a viable alternative
to federal regulation, for several reasons.

First, the legal principles applicable in the states may not be
sufficient to protect competition adequately in many cases. While it
is true that all states have some form of legislation on their books to
protect competition, these laws do not necessarily contain the same
degree of protections for the competitive process as exist under
federal antitrust laws. Moreover, not all states apply their antitrust
laws to the insurance industry. Traditionally, the industry has operated under "mini-McCarran-Ferguson" acts that exempt its activities
from state antitrust regulation as well. Although the current trend is
to repeal these statutes, they continue to exist in a number of states,
and there is no assurance that they will be repealed everywhere.

Second, even where state antitrust law applies and is as stringent
as federal antitrust law, it is not likely to be enforced with nearly the
same efficiency. State antitrust laws are not well developed because
of the overwhelming importance of federal antitrust laws. Thus, in
the absence of federal antitrust scrutiny, the principles that would
apply to the insurance industry would often be uncertain and poorly
understood. Such uncertainty would benefit neither insurance firms
nor consumers. Federal antitrust law, in contrast, is a well-developed
body of law, which, while by no means crystal clear in all details, is

---

[71]672 F.2d at 477.

at least relatively well understood in broad outline.

Third, there exists an extensive and expert bar versed in federal antitrust principles that would aid the industry in compliance and consumers in detecting and remedying violations. A similar bar does not exist in the case of state antitrust regulation. Moreover, the Department of Justice and the Federal Trade Commission possess enormous competence in antitrust regulation and operate with highly trained economists and other experts to assist in complex antitrust enforcement matters. State agencies do not have the same administrative capabilities.

Fourth, insurance markets often extend beyond state boundaries, especially for commercial lines where the market may be regional or even nationwide. In such interstate cases, state regulators may find it difficult to evaluate such factors as geographic market definition or market share analysis when the businesses of the firms involved extend far beyond the state's boundaries. State enforcement of antitrust principles may also run into practical problems because private agreements, boycotts, or restraints can often be sheltered from state scrutiny by being made in other states. Although cooperation among state regulators may mitigate these problems, they nevertheless suggest an additional potential justification for federal antitrust scrutiny. [72]

Conclusions

The McCarran-Ferguson Act should be interpreted to enhance competitive forces in the insurance industry, while not impairing the ability of industry members to engage in socially desirable cooperative activities. The boycott exception to the act should be interpreted to police against the danger of cooperative behavior among firms to coerce others to charge uniform rates, use particular forms, or the like. For similar reasons, the state action immunity should be limited

---

[72]Of course, federal antitrust law would not ordinarily displace state antitrust regulation, which could continue as an adjunct to federal oversight unless preempted. See California v. ARC America Corp., 490 U.S. 93 (1989), holding that state indirect purchaser laws are not preempted by the federal antitrust rule established in Illinois Brick Co. v. Illinois, 431 U.S. 720 (1977), on the ground that "Congress intended the federal antitrust laws to supplement, not displace, state antitrust remedies."

to situations in which the state has actively and continuously regulated the activities in question.

The antitrust laws should not apply, however, to cooperative efforts at sharing and analyzing historical loss cost or prospective loss cost information. Likewise, it is important that firms in the industry have access to standardized forms if they wish to use them. If bona fide activities are threatened by the federal antitrust laws, it may be desirable to implement safe harbors expressly protecting activities where economic benefits clearly outweigh the possible dangers to competition.[73] We believe that appropriately crafted safe harbors could address problems confronting the industry to the extent that the antitrust laws are made applicable to aspects of the business of insurance.[74]

In general, recent interpretations of the McCarran-Ferguson Act have adopted a reasonable construction of the statute. Thus, we do not believe that the act is in need of fundamental modification or repeal. If, however, the statute receives a judicial construction that interferes with the power of the federal antitrust laws to police against threats to competition within the industry, we would then recommend that Congress consider repealing the immunity but at the same time providing explicit safe harbors for economically efficient cooperative activities that do not pose serious threats to competition—such as the sharing and cooperative analysis of historical loss data and prospective loss cost data and the cooperative development of standardized forms.

---

[73]If a safe-harbor approach is adopted, the statute or legislative history should specify that the express mention of certain safe harbors is not in derogation of other permissible cooperative activities, the likely economic benefits of which outweigh the possible dangers to competition.

[74]The safe-harbor approach discussed here resembles a number of recent proposals, including those of the American Bar Association's Commission to Improve the Liability Insurance System, which recommended in 1989 that the antitrust exemption be repealed, subject to a limited authorization "to engage in specified cooperative activity that is shown to enhance the competitiveness of the industry." ABA, *Report of the Commission to Improve the Liability Insurance System*, recommendation 3.1(1)(1989).

4

Solvency Regulation

W E TURN NOW TO THE SECOND major part of this volume,
which considers the impact of the McCarran-Ferguson Act on state
solvency regulation—arguably a more important aspect of the statute
than the better-known antitrust exemption.[1] The adequacy of state
solvency regulation has recently come under attack from several
quarters. The House Energy and Commerce Committee's Subcommittee on Oversight and Investigations has held hearings on insurance
company insolvencies and issued a report, *Failed Promises: Insurance
Company Insolvencies,*[2] popularly known as the Dingell Report.[3] The
General Accounting Office has weighed in with reports criticizing the
existing system of state solvency regulation: the efficacy of the
National Association of Insurance Commissioners is criticized in
*Insurance Regulation: Assessment of the National Association of Insur-
ance Commissioners,*[4] and the vigor of state closure policies comes
under fire in *Insurance Regulation: State Handling of Financially
Troubled Property/Casualty Insurers.*[5] Meanwhile, Public Citizen, a

---

[1]See Spencer Kimball and Barbara Heaney, "Emasculation of the McCarran-
Ferguson Act: A Study in Judicial Activism," *Utah Law Review,* vol. 1
(1985)(eliminating the antitrust exemption would leave the most important part of
the act intact).

[2]House of Representatives, Subcommittee on Oversight and Investigations of the
Committee on Energy and Commerce, *Failed Promises: Insurance Company Insolvencies,* 101st Congress, 2d session (1990).

[3]The Subcommittee on Commerce, Consumer Protection and Competitiveness also
held hearings on the general subject; see *Insurance Company Solvency* (July 17,
1991), and *Life Insurance Guaranty Funds* (July 24, 1991).

[4]Statement of Richard L. Fogel, assistant comptroller general, before the Subcommittee on Oversight and Investigations of the House Committee on Energy and
Commerce, May 22, 1991.

[5]GAO, *Insurance Regulation: State Handling of Troubled Property/Casualty Insurers,*
Report to the Chairwoman, Subcommittee on Commerce, Consumer Protection, and
Competitiveness, House Committee on Energy and Commerce (May 1991).

Nader-affiliated public interest group, announced in October 1990 that five of the top twenty property and casualty firms might fail in the event of an economic downturn. Even though the organization was subsequently forced to retract its charges with respect to several of these firms, the widely publicized allegations reduced consumer confidence in the solvency of the insurance industry as a whole.[6] Even a few voices in the industry itself have expressed a surprising openness to federal solvency regulation.[7]

The Dingell and GAO reports call public attention to the problem of insurance company insolvencies, pointing out a number of regulatory defects at the state level. In our view, however, these reports draw excessive and unwarranted conclusions from the evidence. The insurance industry is not experiencing a solvency crisis. Although there have been widely publicized failures, most insurance firms are solvent and well capitalized. The analogy to the banking industry's insolvency crisis is at best misleading and at worst plainly false. Moreover, states are now proceeding aggressively to improve and strengthen their solvency regulation, which was already relatively well designed before the current round of legislative changes. And any proposals for federalizing state solvency regulation must consider whether the federal government could do a better job at protecting policyholders. Given the shameful failure of the Federal Home Loan Bank Board at preventing the thrift industry from becoming insolvent, there is little reason to suppose that a federal insurance agency would do a better job. In short, the case for federal solvency regulation is not persuasive.[8]

---

[6]See "A Disservice to Public Citizens," *National Underwriter*, November 26, 1990.

[7]The American Insurance Association, representing the larger insurance companies with about 40 percent of the market for commercial lines, has expressed an "open mind" about federal solvency regulation. See Richard L. Hall, "If Solvency Is a Problem, Is Federal Regulation the Solution," *Best's Review*, vol. 91, no. 10 (1991), p. 108.

[8]In this respect our conclusions differ from those contained in MacAvoy, ed., *Federal-State Regulation of the Pricing and Marketing of Insurance*, p. 95. That study—which was conducted well before the failures in the bank and thrift deposit insurance systems of the past few years and the reevaluation of deposit insurance that has followed those financial disasters—recommended some form of federal solvency regulation and also suggested the "probable necessity for a federally established guaranty fund in the event of the sudden, unpredicted demise" of an insurance company doing business under federal auspices.

Current Solvency Conditions

Unquestionably, the insurance industry today is facing solvency problems. The rate of insurance company insolvencies has been rising: there were only eighty-four insolvencies between 1969 and 1983 but fifty-seven insolvencies in the next three years alone. In 1990, twenty-three property and casualty and twenty life insurance firms were declared insolvent, according to NAIC figures.[9] Moreover, some of the recent failures have involved very large firms. The most significant recent failure, that of Mutual Benefit Life, involved a mutual institution with $13.8 billion in assets, one of the larger insurance companies in the nation, representing the largest insurance company failure in American history. The impact of recent failures is vividly illustrated by the figures on assessments from state guaranty funds: between 1969 and 1984, the total assessments on guaranty funds were $393 million; since that time the assessments have approached or exceeded that amount every single year: $323 million (1985), $528 million (1986), $907 million (1987), $452 million (1988), and $775 million (1989).[10] Although there is no indication that the industry has been unable to meet these assessments, the trend toward higher losses is unmistakable.

The failure statistics are matched by decreases in credit ratings. In 1987, 71 percent of the property and casualty companies to which Standard & Poor's assigned a claims-paying–ability rating—in general, the top firms in the industry—were rated AAA; by 1990, only 41 percent received the AAA rating.[11] Standard & Poors' qualified solvency ratings—which are assigned to firms that have not applied for claims-paying–ability ratings—ranked 133 of 633 property and casualty firms at the Bq or below-average rating.[12] Across all lines,

---

[9]Gastel, *Insolvencies/Guaranty Funds*. These are figures provided by the National Association of Insurance Commissioners and do not include small firms doing business only in a single state. Figures from the A. M. Best Company, which do include these small firms, show a total of thirty-two property and casualty insolvencies in 1990.

[10]Ibid.

[11]See Alan Levin, "Financial Uncertainty Ahead for P&C Companies," *National Underwriter*, May 20, 1991.

[12]See ibid. Companies receiving the highest rating, however, wrote 86 percent of the total premiums.

489 insurers out of 1,600 received the Bq rating.[13] Moody's Investors Service downgraded the credit ratings of a number of life insurance firms, including some of the industry's largest institutions.[14]

The reasons for the insurance company insolvencies are not difficult to find. In many respects, they are similar to the problems plaguing the banking industry: heavy investment in commercial real estate that has undergone the most dramatic deflation in prices since the Depression[15] and large investments by some life insurance companies in junk bonds that have soured.[16] According to one recent study, the ratio of high-risk assets (junk bonds and troubled real estate investments) to total surplus (statutory surplus plus mandatory

---

[13]Judy Greenwald, "S&P Rebuffs Criticism: Company Contends New Solvency Ratings Are Fair," *Business Insurance*, April 22, 1991, p. 2.

[14]The downgraded firms included Aetna Life & Casualty Co., Crown Life Insurance Co., Kemper Corp., Home Life Insurance Co., Travelers Corp., John Hancock Mutual Life, Massachusetts Mutual, Principal Mutual, Mutual Life Insurance Company of New York, and New England Mutual Life Insurance. See "Moody's Cuts Ratings on Four Insurance Companies," *Reuters Business Report*, July 26, 1991; Nikki Tait, "Moody's Downgrades Six US Insurers," *Financial Times*, July 22, 1991.

[15]The actual number of firms with serious real estate problems is relatively small, however; as of April 1991, only about a dozen life insurance firms had mortgage problems and defaults in excess of 40 percent of surplus. Gil Marmol and John Shuck, "Testing the Mettle of Life Insurers, *Best's Review*, vol. 91, no. 12, p. 16. These firms, however, included some of the major companies in the industry. The industry's total investment in real estate has decreased steadily since 1966, when mortgages constituted 38.6 percent of the assets of life insurance firms, to 1989, when mortgages represented only 19.5 percent of life insurance assets. American Council of Life Insurance, *1990 Life Insurance Fact Book*, p. 94. Real estate owned outright has remained at very close to 3 percent of assets since 1960. See ibid., p. 98.

[16]Virtually all the junk bond exposure is in the life insurance sector; casualty and property firms did not buy large volumes of high-yield debt and had only 1 percent of assets in junk bonds at year-end 1988. See Russ Banham, "Junk Jitters," *Insurance Review*, vol. 51, no. 4 (April 1990), p. 9. Even within the life sector, the number of firms with heavy exposure in junk bonds is small, although the firms involved are substantial in terms of assets. As of April 1991, it was estimated that thirty-seven life insurance companies, accounting for 16 percent of the industry's invested assets, had junk bond portfolios in excess of 100 percent of surplus; twelve companies had junk bond portfolios in excess of 200 percent of surplus. Marmol and Shuck, "Testing the Mettle of Life Insurers." In total, however, only 4.8 percent of the assets of life insurance companies were invested in junk bonds.

securities valuation reserve) jumped from 91 percent in 1989 to 140 percent in 1990.[17] The problems of the savings and loans have also spilled over into the insurance industry to some extent; one source estimates that insurance company payments under directors' and officers' liability insurance policies in litigation brought by receivers of failed depository institutions may eventually total $200 million.[18]

At the same time, there is no reason at present to suppose that the insurance industry as a whole will experience the sorts of catastrophic failures that have recently occurred in the thrift and commercial banking industries. The two industries are not similarly situated, for a number of reasons.

Insurance firms are not constrained by the restrictive asset rules that apply to banks and thrift institutions and therefore are better able to diversify their investment portfolios. In particular, many insurance firms are allowed to invest some of their portfolios in equity securities.[19] Junk bonds, therefore, had less appeal to insurance companies because they could seek high returns in equity markets, a strategy foreclosed to banks and thrift institutions. The strong stock market bolstered the insurance industry's investment returns at a time when some junk bond portfolios were performing badly.[20]

Unlike banks and thrifts, insurance companies do not offer risk-free investments that can be marketed nationwide and used to expand the size of fundamentally unsound institutions and stave off failure. Because of the federal deposit guarantee and the highly liquid nature of bank deposit accounts, many banks and thrifts used the services of deposit brokers to expand their deposit bases and grow dramatically in size and then invested the deposited funds in unsound or highly speculative ventures. Many of these fast-growing depository institutions have subsequently failed. This strategy is not readily

---

[17]Frederick S. Townsend, "High Risk Assets: 140% of Total Surplus," *National Underwriter*, June 3, 1991, p. 3.

[18]Gastel, *Financial and Market Conditions.*

[19]As of 1989, life insurance companies invested 9.7 percent of their total assets in corporate equity securities. American Council of Life Insurance, *1990 Life Insurance Fact Book*, p. 83.

[20]During the first quarter of 1991, for example, investment income for property and casualty insurance companies increased 6.8 percent over the same quarter of 1990, driven largely by a 19.1 percent increase in capital gains realized mostly in stock markets. Gastel, *Financial and Market Conditions.*

available to insurance firms, because the insurance product is neither risk free nor as liquid as bank certificates of deposit. Some insurance firms offered investment vehicles such as annuity contracts in the 1980s and attempted to grow quickly by offering cheap premiums, but this group represents only a small segment of the market— although a large percentage of the insurance companies that have failed[21]—and in any event was not as effective in this strategy as the "high-flying" savings and loan institutions. Thus, even if an insurance firm were inclined to adopt a risky investment strategy, it could not leverage a federal deposit guarantee into an indefinite expansion, with the expense of the expansion ultimately borne by the taxpayers.

The troubles of the insurance industry are not nearly as severe as those that until recently characterized the banking industry. Although a few firms have failed, the failures have not been dramatic and affected only a small percentage—less than 1 percent in 1990— of the total firms in the industry.[22] The failures that have occurred do not appear to have involved the sort of catastrophic insolvencies that have plagued the thrift industry.

Some firms commonly considered to have failed, such as Mutual Benefit Life and Monarch Life, may not have been economically insolvent at the time of their closure and may eventually pay out creditors in full.[23] These early closures reflect the fact that the insurance industry is handling its problems more effectively than the

---

[21]The growth patterns of firms involved in some of the most prominent recent failures are illustrative. Executive Life Insurance Company of California grew from $4 billion in assets in 1984 to $13 billion in 1989, largely through the sale of annuity contracts. See *Best's Insurance Reports* (Life-Health) (1990), p. 751. Executive Life Insurance Company of New York grew from $1.7 billion in assets in 1984 to $3.9 billion in 1989, ibid., p. 755. The Mutual Benefit Life Insurance Company did not adopt a high-growth strategy until very shortly before its failure, with admitted assets growing from $8.3 billion in 1984 to $11.6 billion in 1989, ibid., p. 1523. Mutual Benefit Life, however, did appear to adopt a high-growth strategy after 1989, with individual life insurance in force growing from $36.3 billion in 1989 to $67.3 billion in 1990, an increase of 85.4 percent in a single year. Jim Connolly, "Larger Cos. Showed Growth across the Board," *National Underwriter*, June 10, 1991, p. S2.

[22]See Gastel, *Insolvencies/Guaranty Funds*.

[23]See "New Jersey Court Appoints Conservator of Troubled Mutual Benefit Life Insurance," *BNA Pension Reporter*, vol. 18, no. 29 (July 22, 1991), p. 1240; Jim Connolly, "Penn Mutual Is Monarch's New Manager," *National Underwriter*, June 24, 1991, p. 29.

banking industry has done. Early closure can prevent or, at the very least, mitigate creditors' losses. If banks and insurance companies could be closed before insolvency, creditors' losses would be nonexistent.

The recent downgrading in credit ratings for major life insurance firms, while receiving widespread publicity, in fact did not reflect extraordinary weaknesses in these firms; even after the downgrades, most of the affected firms were considered to be in good or excellent financial health.[24] Moody's emphasized that the "vast majority" of rated insurance companies continued to be of "exceptional," "excellent," or "good" financial strength.[25]

Moreover, as far as is possible to predict, the rate of failures is not likely to increase substantially. The commercial real estate market, while still depressed, has begun to recover. Blue-chip equity securities are trading at record levels.

The insurance industry as a whole is not suffering losses in capital.[26] Moreover, the industry appears to have relatively good access to new capital. Capital can be generated internally by retaining earnings rather than paying dividends. Property and casualty firms, for example, paid out $4.9 billion in dividends in 1988,[27] some of which could have been retained to increase capital; life insurance firms paid out over $5 billion in dividends in 1989.[28] Stock firms can also raise equity capital by selling new securities on the market. Parent corporations can and do infuse new capital into insurance subsidiaries.[29] Mutual institutions, which have been among

---

[24]See Tait, "Moody's Downgrades Six US Insurers." Even after the recent downgrades, only one of the nation's twenty biggest insurance firms—Mutual Life Insurance Company of New York—received a Moody's rating below the "A" level, which implies "exceptional," "excellent," or "good." MONY received a "Baa-1," meaning "adequate." See Richard D. Hylton, "MONY, Sorely Tested, Reassures Customers," *New York Times*, August 2, 1991.

[25]See *Reuters Financial Report*, July 19, 1991.

[26]See Gastel, *Financial and Market Conditions: Property/Casualty Insurance*; American Council of Life Insurance, *1990 Life Insurance Fact Book*, (1990) p. 81.

[27]See *1990 Property/Casualty Insurance Facts*, p. 2.

[28]See American Council of Life Insurance, *1990 Life Insurance Fact Book* (1990), p. 75.

[29]Recently, for example, Kemper Corp. committed $1.8 billion in capital to back the operations of two life insurance subsidiaries that had been downgraded by

the hardest hit by recent economic conditions, are increasingly considering demutualization—converting to stock ownership—as a means of increasing capital.[30] Demutualization will increase the capitalization of insurance firms, especially in the life insurance industry where mutual firms are heavily represented. On balance, there is little reason to suppose that, in the absence of unforeseeable external factors such as a stock market crash, a new round of recession, or a natural catastrophe (such as Hurricane Hugo), the insurance industry will experience a major reduction in capital over the next few years.

If the federal antitrust laws were applied to the business of insurance, the result might ultimately be to increase the rate of failures of insurance firms because of the increase in competition brought about by the repeal of the antitrust exemption. But an increase in failures of insurance firms should not be a cause for excessive worry. The possibility of failure is the price that a market system pays for the enhanced quality and productivity—and benefits to the consumer—that competition induces in an industry. The states would be well advised to scrutinize insurance company capital carefully and to close institutions—or force mergers with better-capitalized firms—before the point of actual economic insolvency, to protect the interests of policyholders. An increase in insurance company failures due to application of the federal antitrust law should not, however, be taken as evidence of any need for comprehensive federal regulation outside the antitrust field.

A recent study of the industry by Orin Kramer bears out these conclusions as applied to property and casualty firms.[31] Kramer finds that an industrywide solvency crisis for the insurance industry is improbable, even under pessimistic economic assumptions. In gen-

---

Moody's Investors Service, Inc. See Laurie Cohen, "Kemper Backs Its 2 Life Units," *Chicago Tribune*, July 28, 1991. This action came on the heels of a prior injection of $125 million in additional capital into the companies.

[30]Leading this movement is the Equitable Life Assurance Society of the U.S., which recently converted from a mutual to a stock institution and which received a commitment from an investor to infuse $1 billion in new capital into the firm even before the planned public stock offering. See Susan Pulliam, "Equitable Life's Plan to Sell Stake Advances," *Wall Street Journal*, July 18, 1991. The investor is the French insurance firm Groupe Axa, S.A.

[31]Orin Kramer, *Rating the Risks: Assessing the Solvency Threat in the Financial Services Industry* (Washington, D.C.: Insurance Information Institute, 1991).

eral, Kramer finds that property and casualty firms, including the weakest segment of this industry, are relatively strong compared with counterparts in other industrial sectors.

State Solvency Regulation

State solvency regulation of insurance companies has three main features: regulatory safety and soundness supervision, minimum capital rules, and guaranty funds. For the most part, these regulations appear relatively well crafted to achieve their objectives. Moreover, states are now proceeding vigorously to strengthen their solvency regulations. The National Conference of State Legislators established a task force on insurance solvency regulation in 1990 and announced that enactment of tougher laws would be a high priority.[32] The NAIC, meanwhile, has implemented solvency accreditation standards, under which state regulators, to receive certification, must establish that they have adequate powers under state law and that they have the necessary resources to enforce them.[33] The NAIC is proceeding rapidly to evaluate state regulatory agencies under this program and may adopt tougher regulations at some point under which insurers in states failing to adopt the NAIC's model insolvency laws will be penalized.[34] The NAIC has also announced its own priorities for toughening solvency regulation.[35]

Safety and Soundness Regulation. All state regulatory systems place restrictions on the sorts of assets in which an insurance company can invest. Until recently, there were few restrictions on the power of insurance firms to purchase corporate debt securities. This left insurance firms free to purchase high-yield ("junk") bonds for

---

[32]See Gastel, *Insolvencies/Guaranty Funds.*

[33]See ibid.

[34]See ibid.

[35]See ibid. The priorities include "refining the financial examination process; expanding the information provided in annual statement on material transactions; creating a reinsurance office to assist states in the evaluation of reinsurance companies and contracts; upgrading training programs for financial analysts, auditors and regulators; and setting up a special committee to study the receivership process as it applies to insolvent insurance companies."

their portfolios, and a number of insurance firms have invested heavily in these securities.

Investments in junk bonds have been said to reflect lax safety and soundness supervision. It should be remembered, however, that junk bonds, while they may appear to be unsound investments today, did not necessarily appear unsound at the time in which the insurance companies made their investments. Many individuals and institutions purchased junk bonds in the 1980s with full awareness that these investments carried substantial risk, but with the considered judgment that the high returns promised on the securities more than offset the risks. Limited investments in diversified portfolios of junk bonds were perfectly appropriate for insurance companies, even if the investments have not always turned out as well as the investment strategists hoped. Similarly, while in retrospect it is easy to say that state insurance regulators should have intervened sooner to prevent accumulation of junk bond portfolios by life insurance firms, this failure appears less egregious when viewed from the perspective of the times. State regulators (perhaps unwisely) are now moving to restrict insurance company purchases of junk bonds to prevent a recurrence of the problem.[36]

In addition to imposing restrictions on investments, state insurance regulators monitor the safety of institutions under their jurisdiction by means of site examinations and analyses of report data. Insurance firms are required to file annual financial statements with their regulators. State regulators examine the data by use of systems developed by the NAIC.[37]

State regulators conduct more detailed investigations of firms identified as potential problems by the NAIC. If the problems prove to be serious, insurance regulators take a series of increasingly severe remedial actions, ranging from intensive audits to private persuasion

---

[36]See ibid.

[37]Economists have criticized the NAIC's analysis for failing to predict insolvency reliably. See, for example, Robert A. Hershbarger and Ronald K. Miller, "The NAIC Information System and the Use of Economic Indicators in Predicting Insolvencies," *Journal of Insurance Issues and Practices*, vol. 9 (1986), p. 21. Somewhat greater predictive accuracy can apparently be achieved with highly sophisticated models; see Ran B'arNiv and Hershbarger, "Classifying Financial Distress in the Life Insurance Industry," *Journal of Risk and Insurance*, vol. 57 (1990), p. 110, although none of the models proposed to date appear particularly robust.

in minor cases to formal orders requiring the firm to improve its solvency by increasing capital or restructuring its investments, to public remedial actions such as placing the institution in conservatorship or rehabilitation. The ultimate step is receivership and liquidation.

Minimum Capital Rules. All states require that insurance firms licensed to do business in the state operate with specified levels of minimum capital or surplus for the payment of policyholders' claims as they arise. As a practical matter, primary responsibility for determining a firm's level of capital and surplus is left to the insurance commissioner in the state of the company's domicile. Other state regulators, however, retain the power to bar firms from writing policies in their states if they conclude that a given institution lacks the capital or surplus that a particular regulator deems necessary to provide adequate protection for policyholders.

Guaranty Funds. Every state has established a guaranty fund covering policyholders in homeowners, automobile, and other property and casualty companies,[38] and all but a few have similar programs in place for life and health insurance companies.[39] Most states have workers' compensation funds. Other lines such as disability, ocean marine, mortgage guaranty, and title insurance are less fully covered. Reinsurance is generally not covered. The state guaranty funds have mostly been created over the past two decades on a model proposed by the NAIC in 1969. The funds differ in details such as deductibles, policy limits, and the like. Some states deny coverage to larger corporate policyholders, on the theory that these sophisticated consumers can assess the solvency of insurance firms on their own.[40]

The great majority of these state guaranty funds operate on an assessment system: there is no permanent fund in place, but partici-

---

[38]See Gastel, *Insolvencies/Guaranty Funds.*

[39]See ibid. New Jersey adopted such a program on an emergency basis in response to the failure of Mutual Benefit Life. See "Legislation Enacted Creating Fund to Cover Benefits for Failed Insurers," *BNA Pension Reporter,* vol. 18, no. 29, p. 1241 (July 22, 1991).

[40]See Gastel, *Insolvencies/Guaranty Funds.*

pating insurance companies are assessed to cover payments to policyholders that are not covered by the assets of a failed institution.[41] Assessments are typically paid either through state-mandated premium increases—in which case the costs are automatically passed on to policyholders in the form of higher prices—or by tax relief for the insurance companies, in which case the effective cost of the assessments is passed to the state's taxpayers.[42] New York, a major insurance market as well as home for many of the largest insurance firms, is an exception: it has established a permanent fund like those in bank deposit insurance schemes.[43] At least one of the state assessment systems (Maine's) includes a limited permanent fund for the payment of policyholders, pending collection of assessments.[44]

Additional legislation on guaranty funds can be expected in the coming years. One sensible proposal is to base assessments on some criterion of risk rather than on the basis of market share as under current law.[45] As we have noted in other work, a guaranty system that does not adjust premiums for risk induces distortions by providing a subsidy for riskier institutions at the expense of safer ones.[46] The absence (until recently) of risk-based deposit insurance premiums has been a principal culprit in the current debacle in the banking industry, and similar distortions are undoubtedly introduced into insurance markets as a result of the flat-rate premium structure under state guaranty systems.

In endorsing risk-adjusted premiums, we do not mean to imply that it will be easy to determine risk. Evaluating the riskiness of an insurance firm—especially a property and casualty firm—is difficult

---

[41]See ibid. The assessments are collected through changes in premium tax rates, insurance policy surcharges, or changes in premium rates.

[42]See General Accounting Office, *Insurance Regulation: State Handling of Financially Troubled Property/Casualty Insurers* (1991), p. 12. In the case of property and casualty firms, thirty-one states authorize the recoupment of assessments through premium increases; seventeen authorize recoupment through tax relief; one allows either method; and one provides for no method of recoupment.

[43]See Gastel, *Insolvencies/Guaranty Funds.*

[44]See ibid.

[45]See ibid.

[46]See Jonathan R. Macey and Geoffrey P. Miller, "America's Banking System: The Origins and Future of the Current Crisis," *Washington University Law Quarterly*, vol. 69 (1991), p. 769.

because neither the demands for payment on the liability side of its balance sheet (policyholders' claims) nor the value or volatility of the assets held on the asset side of the balance sheet is readily quantified. There are, however, several sources of information about the riskiness of insurance firms. One agency, A. M. Best, has long published ratings for all firms in the industry, and recently the Standard & Poor's Corporation has entered the field with its own credit-rating system for all firms, not just those submitting to claims-paying–ability review. Moody's also rates many larger insurance firms. Although the reliability of these rating systems is not firmly established, they clearly provide useful information on which at least a tentative assessment of risk can be based.[47] Also potentially valuable in assessing risk is the level of capital in an insurance company. Other things being equal, the more capital a firm has, the

---

[47]The 1990 edition of *Best's Insurance Reports* characterized Mutual Benefit Life as "most ably managed" in "the highest ideals of business equity" and gave the firm its highest rating of "A+ (superior)," *Best's Insurance Reports* (Life-Health), pp. 1521–23. Best's downgraded Mutual Benefit Life to a "Contingent A" a few days before it was closed, citing "uncertainties surrounding the timing and ultimate success of the company's repositioning plan and capital raising effort," Cynthia Crosson,"Mut. Benefit's A.M. Best Rating Drops One Notch," *National Underwriter*, July 15, 1991, p. 19. Standard and Poor's gave Mutual Benefit Life an "A" rating for overall financial health and claims-paying ability up until a few days before the failure. See "New Jersey Court Appoints Conservator of Troubled Mutual Benefit Life," *BNA Pension Reporter*, vol. 18, no. 29 (July 22, 1991), p. 1240. Moody's also gave Mutual Benefit Life an "A3" rating (the lower part of the "good" category) and only downgraded it thirteen notches to "Caa" a few days before its failure. See "Moody's Cuts Mutual Benefit Rating," *Reuters Financial Report*, July 15, 1991. In fairness, it should be noted that the earlier, favorable ratings were not necessarily erroneous, since Mutual Benefit Life failed as a result of a policyholder run rather than any determination of insolvency. See Eric N. Berg, "Insurers' Raters Are on the Spot for Inaccuracy," *New York Times*, August 4, 1991.

The rating agencies did somewhat better in the case of other prominent failures. In the case of Executive Life Insurance Company of New York, Best's identified several of the weaknesses that precipitated its eventual failure, including losses from its large junk bond portfolio and increased surrenders and withdrawal activity by policyholders. The ultimate rating, however, was "Contingent A (Excellent)." See ibid, pp. 753–55. The Executive Life Insurance Company (in California) also received a "Contingent A (Excellent)," with the Best's report assuring readers that "actuarial studies indicate that even under a considerable economic downturn whereby significant fluctuations in interest rates and increased default rates would be experienced, together with accelerated surrender and withdrawal activity on the part of First Executive's policyholders, adequate liquidity is maintained to meet any further adverse experience in these areas." Ibid., pp. 749–51.

safer it is. And capital levels can be further developed to account for the riskiness of the assets against which the capital is held. Risk-adjusted deposit insurance premiums for banks based on a measure of risk-adjusted capital are a sensible, if partial, solution to the perverse incentives credited by deposit insurance;[48] although not without problems, a similar measure of risk-adjusted capital might prove useful in setting premium rates for insurance firms.[49]

Another proposal, which strikes us as less sound, is to convert the existing assessment systems into prefunded plans like New York's.[50] The advantage of a prefunded system is that the money is available immediately to meet policyholders' claims. Immediate availability of funds reduces the disruption and hardship to policy-holders, who would otherwise have to wait until the completion of an assessment before obtaining their funds. In the case of life insurance firms, a prefunded system also reduces the danger of runs by policyholders with rights to cash in the investment value of their policies on demand.[51]

Despite these advantages, a prefunded system has serious drawbacks. First, it creates a fund that can thereafter be used to support government activities not reasonably related to solvency regulation or to bail out firms not originally participating in the fund. Second, once a well-capitalized fund is in place, insurance companies lose some of their incentive to police their peers to prevent assessments.[52] Moreover, a prefunded plan reduces monitoring in-

---

[48]See U.S. Department of the Treasury, *Modernizing the Financial System: Recommendations for Safer, More Competitive Banks* (Washington, D.C.: GPO, 1991).

[49]See Macey and Miller, "America's Banking System."

[50]See Gastel, *Insolvencies/Guaranty Funds.*

[51]Such a run occurred in the case of Mutual Benefit Life in July 1991 and precipitated the failure of that institution. It should be noted, however, that New Jersey did not have a guaranty law in effect for life insurance firms at the time. It is unclear whether policyholders would have run the institution if an assessment type of guaranty law had been on the books. Further, the danger that a solvent company would have to close because of a run would be much reduced if, as we recommend in this volume, the Federal Reserve is brought into service as lender of last resort for the insurance industry.

[52]As a practical matter, insurance companies retain a fair degree of ability to police their peers. A firm reputed in the industry to be managed in an excessively risky or improper manner may find it difficult to obtain adequate reinsurance, for example. If the firm uses independent agents for distribution, it may find that agents

centives by the parties that would be liable for assessments under an assessment system.[53] If the federal deposit guaranty program had been an assessment system rather than a richly endowed (before 1985) prefunded plan, it is possible that the well-managed and solvent banks and thrift institutions would have organized to prevent the excessive risk taking by others in the industry, which eventuated in the current crisis in the banking industry.[54]

A third consideration suggesting the advantage of assessment systems over prefunded plans is that some of the advantages of prefunded plans can be achieved through suitable modifications in assessment plans. Most states, for example, now allow policyholders

---

are loath to recommend its product to customers. See "Producers and Insolvencies," *National Underwriter*, May 28, 1990, p. 44. (Insurance regulators want brokers and agents to provide them with information about the financial health of insurance firms and to exercise due diligence and reasonable care when placing insurance with a company.) Insurance firms also exercise influence with state insurance regulators and may encourage the regulators to take prompt action to resolve insurance firms that others in the industry believe to be unsafe or unsound.

[53]Of course, even in a prefunded plan, the parties required to replenish the fund in the event of payouts retain some monitoring incentive. If the fund is solvent enough, however, it may effectively replenish itself through investment income. And even if some assessments are made, the existence of a fund for the payment of assessments contributes to a breakage in the connection between the failure of an insurance company and the liability of another to pay an assessment. Reduced monitoring incentives are the result.

[54]Along these same lines, we question why under existing state plans, assessments should be paid by means of premium increases or—worse—by tax relief for insurance firms. These payment methods operate virtually invisibly and pass the incidence of the assessments on to groups that are not well equipped to monitor the behavior of insurance firms in the state—policyholders and taxpayers. To induce optimal monitoring and mitigate the incentives for risk taking that are built into any fixed-premium insurance system, the assessments ought to run against parties well equipped to engage in appropriate monitoring. These parties are other insurance firms in the state. Rather than being paid wholly by policyholders or taxpayers, assessments should be paid partly by the insurance firms covered by the guaranty fund, in proportion to the volume of business conducted by the firm in the state, with suitable adjustment for the riskiness of the firm being assessed. Moreover, to the extent that assessments are paid out of tax dollars, rather than from insurance companies directly, it would be better for these funds to be obtained from taxpayers in some relatively public manner calculated to induce political accountability, rather than through the nearly invisible method of tax relief for insurance companies, as is the case under current state guaranty systems.

early access to the assets of a failed institution ahead of the claims of other creditors.[55] Maine has created a limited prefunded plan to pay off policyholders in the short run; this approach may draw a more reasonable balance between the need to pay off policyholders quickly and the value of peer group monitoring that assessment plans provide.

Resolution of Insolvencies. Once an insurance firm has become insolvent, state regulators use a variety of mechanisms to resolve the problem and pay off creditors in the order of their priority. For the most part, insurance insolvencies resemble banking insolvencies. As in the case of banking insolvencies, a fiduciary is appointed to handle the affairs of the failed institution. If there is a good chance the institution can be returned to solvency without liquidation, it may be placed in conservatorship and allowed to continue in business under close regulatory supervision. More severe cases where return to solvency is still a possibility are sometimes handled through rehabilitation, which is an arrangement under which the regulator, for all intents and purposes, operates the institution. If the company is deemed unsalvageable, it will be liquidated under the control of a receiver.

These procedures are subject to some of the same problems that have troubled bank insolvencies. In particular, the availability of conservatorships and rehabilitation creates a danger that failing but politically powerful firms (and many insurance companies are well connected in statehouses and with state insurance regulators) will seek regulatory forbearance to avoid liquidation. In the case of the banking industry, political pressures for regulatory forbearance triggered the notorious scandals involving Speaker of the House Jim Wright and the "Keating five" senators who intervened with regulators, allegedly improperly, to stave off regulatory action against the embarrassed depository institution.

Similar dangers attend insurance insolvencies, although to date there have been no disclosures of major improprieties. The General Accounting Office's study found, however, that

insurance regulators were typically late in taking formal action against financially troubled companies. State regulators did

---

[55]See Gastel, *Insolvencies/Guaranty Funds.*

not take formal action in 71 percent of failed insurer cases for which data were available until the insurers became insolvent or later. In at least thirty-six failed insurer cases, insurers continued to write policies after regulators identified them as financially troubled.[56]

The GAO attributed the regulatory delay to factors such as "reliance on untimely or unverified information," "lack of legal or regulatory standards for defining a troubled insurer," and "a vague and unspecific statutory definition of insolvency."[57] The GAO report does not mention the additional possibility that political pressures may have induced regulatory delay, but the existence of such pressures seems possible in some cases.

The GAO report raises valid concerns about state solvency regulation. As we have already noted, however, the same concerns have plagued federal resolution procedures. Moreover, a promising approach to the problem of late closure—statutory standards mandating early regulatory intervention—has been suggested at the federal level for the depository institution insurance funds; there seems little reason why similar early closure regulations could not be adopted at the state level as well.

On balance, state insurance regulators have done a good job ensuring the safety and soundness of firms under their supervision. The insurance industry survived the economic shocks and dislocations of the 1980s in far better condition than the commercial banking sector, even though insurance, unlike banking, lacks a safety net in the form of federal deposit insurance. There is no solvency crisis in the industry, and the problems, such as they are, have been identified and are being addressed. There is no affirmative case for federal regulation based on serious shortfalls in the system of state solvency regulation.

Models of Federal Regulation

We now consider a number of proposals currently circulating that would subject the insurance industry to federal oversight to one

---

[56]General Accounting Office, *Insurance Regulation: State Handling of Financially Troubled Property/Casualty Insurers* (Washington, D.C.: GPO, 1991), p. 3.

[57]Ibid.

92

degree or another. We also discuss our own suggestion for a limited federal role as lender of last resort to the industry.

Federal Solvency Regulation. A proposal recently aired on Capitol Hill would create a federal insurance agency with broad powers to displace state regulatory authority.[58] This proposal, promoted most prominently by Congessman John Dingell, would establish a federal insurer solvency corporation, which would have the authority to supervise the industry's self-regulatory organizations (SROs). An approved SRO could have the authority to authorize an insurance company to conduct an interstate business, apparently free of the substantive regulation of any state of domicile. The result would be a form of federal chartering of insurance and could create a structure for the insurance business similar to the dual banking system now in place for depository institutions.[59] The federal regulator would set minimum standards for fundamental matters such as accounting, investment, capital, and surplus, which states would have to equal or exceed to be accredited to regulate insurers in interstate commerce. The federal regulator would also exercise authority over the reinsurance business and could close insolvent or shaky insurance companies.

The Dingell proposal would essentially federalize insurance regulation, subject only to vestigial state regulatory oversight. If enacted, it would most probably lead to the eventual atrophy of state insurance oversight except in the key area of rate regulation, which would be explicitly left to state control under current versions of the proposal. Unlike other forms of regulation, state rate regulation would likely increase in stringency under the Dingell proposal, for several reasons. Deprived of most other authority, state insurance regulators would be likely to return aggressively to rate regulation as a means of maintaining some of their traditional powers. Expanded rate regulation would also offer the opportunity for the industry to bring

---

[58]See Frederick Rose, "Congressional Proposals on Insurance Would End Primacy of State Regulation," *Wall Street Journal*, August 5, 1991.

[59]For background on the dual banking system, see Butler and Macey, "The Myth of Competition in the Dual Banking System," p. 101; Geoffrey Miller, "The Future of the Dual Banking System," *Brooklyn Law Review*, vol. 53 (1987), p. 1; Kenneth Scott, "The Dual Banking System: A Model of Competition in Regulation," *Stanford Law Review*, vol. 30 (1977), p. 1.

cooperative price-setting activities within the shelter of the state action doctrine, as discussed earlier. Some consumer groups would also favor substantive rate regulation as a means of rolling back rates they consider too high. Moreover, in an environment of federal solvency regulation, states might see the benefit of forcing below-market rates on insurers on the theory that customers in other states will make up the shortfall and the federal government will ensure that firms do not fail.

Federal Guaranty Fund. Senator Howard Metzenbaum has recommended the creation of a federal guaranty fund for insurance policyholders, which would displace the existing state guaranty funds.[60] This idea, in our view, is also flawed. As the catastrophes over the past five years in the two principal guaranty funds for banking institutions, the Bank Insurance Fund and the Federal Savings and Loan Insurance Corporation, have shown, the last thing the federal government should do is enter another open-ended contingent obligation with an enormous potential risk exposure. Concern about federal budget deficits alone should cause the concept of a vast new program of federal insurance guarantees to be greeted with horror. This is particularly true since there is no reason to believe that a federal insurance fund will be any less subject to the problems of moral hazard and perverse incentives that doomed the federal deposit insurance funds.

Further, it seems clear that, to the extent that guaranty funds exist at all, they are better administered at the state level than by a federal agency. It should be noted that most state guaranty funds cover only in-state depositors. This limitation in coverage creates a system in which insurance regulators in other states have a strong incentive to monitor the solvency regulation of a company's domiciliary state to reduce the claims on their own insurance guaranty systems. The advantages of monitoring one state's regulator by other regulators in other states would be lost if state guaranty schemes were displaced by a single federal insurance fund.

Moreover, a federal guaranty system would further aggravate the temptation of some states to expropriate the wealth of citizens of other

---

[60]See Rose, "Congressional Proposals on Insurance Would End Primacy of State Regulation."

states by imposing below-market rates. In an interesting recent paper, economist Benjamin Zycher explores the probable impact of federal solvency regulation on state rate setting.[61] Zycher observes that if the federal government were to regulate the solvency of insurance companies by displacing state guaranty programs with a federal guaranty fund, state rate-setting bodies would inevitably face irresistible political pressure to set rates below the market-clearing rate. By setting low rates, states could benefit their own citizens at the expense of insurance firms and the federal guaranty fund. Eventually, some of the insurance firms would fail as a result of continuing losses, but the costs of the failure would be borne by the federal insurance fund. As in the banking industry, the result of federal intervention would be to impair the solvency of the insurance industry. It would also restrict the supply of insurance, thus harming the policyholders it was ostensibly designed to protect. Zycher observes that these perverse regulatory results would not occur if solvency regulation were administered by the states, since then interests within a state would bear the costs of the state's setting insurance rates at unreasonably low rates.

These considerations suggest that a federal guaranty program for insurance policyholders would be ill advised. They also imply that if such a program were adopted, the administrator of the federal guaranty fund would inevitably become involved in rate regulation. To protect the assets of the guaranty fund, the federal administrator would have to supervise the safety and soundness of the institutions under the fund; and safety and soundness supervision cannot be accomplished effectively if states maintain plenary control over rate setting. Thus federal guarantees would broaden into generalized federal oversight of the substance of state regulation, including state rate regulation. The notion of a dual system with a federal guaranty fund and state regulation of the business of insurance outside the solvency area is, accordingly, unstable, leading eventually to broader, preemptive federal oversight of many aspects of the insurance business.

Interstate Compact. A more appealing model of federal involvement in the insurance industry is the possibility that the states might

---

[61]Benjamin Zycher, "Insurance Rates, Direct Democracy and Solvency Regulation" (paper on file with the authors, 1991).

enhance their ability to supervise national insurance companies by entering an interstate compact, subject to the federal oversight that would flow from the requirement that any such interstate compact must receive congressional approval.[62]

A leading proponent of the interstate compact idea is James M. Jackson, vice president and deputy general counsel of Transamerica Life Insurance Co. He describes the idea as follows:

> By utilizing the "compact clause" of the federal constitution . . . the states have the power to institute any uniform standards, rules, and enforcement mechanisms deemed necessary and appropriate. . . . An interstate compact occupies a position of overriding authority with respect to other statutory law, whether previously or subsequently adopted. The reason . . . is that in addition to being [a] statute, an interstate compact also constitutes an enforceable contract among all the states which become party to it. . . . Compacts thus provide a constitutional, statutory, and contractual basis for uniform state regulation.[63]

An interstate compact would theoretically permit the NAIC—or some other body chosen by the states as a central regulator—to exercise a degree of compulsory authority over the separate state insurance departments. This would be a significant increase in power in comparison with the present situation, in which NAIC is a purely voluntary organization, exercising persuasive authority but without the power to compel a state regulator or an insurance company to take any particular action.

An interstate compact could establish a national association of state insurance regulators with powers to centralize information gathering and retrieval functions and to promulgate uniform rules in areas where interstate differences pose special difficulties. Such a national association could, for example, compile and maintain information about the financial condition of insurance firms on a nationwide basis; it could establish uniform standards for insurance companies in financial difficulty, requiring regulatory intervention; it could assist in administering receiverships of failed institutions that

---

[62]See U.S. Constitution, Article I, section 10, clause 2.

[63]James M. Jackson, "A New Dimension for State Regulation," *National Underwriter*, November 19, 1990, p. 21.

operate interstate; and it could even issue uniform capital adequacy standards for firms doing business across state lines.

Lender of Last Resort. Finally, we come to a form of federal oversight that we believe would be a desirable addition to the current regulatory system: the establishment of the Federal Reserve as a lender of last resort for the insurance industry. The recent failures of Mutual Benefit Life Insurance Company and several other firms brought to public attention the fact that many life insurance companies operate with the equivalent of demand or near-demand debt in their balance sheets. Policyholders can liquidate the cash value of their annuities and guaranteed investment contracts on demand or after only a brief notice period.[64] This demand and near-demand debt creates the possibility of runs based on information, or misinformation, that the company is in financial straits. The exposure of some life insurance firms to this kind of run is very large,[65] and has induced major rating firms to consider the risk of runs as a factor in their evaluation of insurance firms' credit.[66]

Property and casualty firms are subject to a related but slightly different risk. A major earthquake or other extraordinary disaster could result in tens of billions of dollars of claims being made on the assets of property and casualty firms within a very short time. Faced with these claims, the firms would be required to liquidate their assets rapidly, resulting in "fire-sale" losses. Some firms with relatively illiquid asset portfolios might be unable to pay out claims when due. Regulators might be required to close firms as a result, even though those firms might be perfectly solvent if given adequate time to liquidate their assets in an orderly fashion.

These considerations suggest the value of a lender of last resort for the insurance industry—an entity that could advance temporary liquidity assistance to solvent firms to tide them over until they could liquidate sufficient assets to pay off the demands of policyholders.

---

[64]See Eric N. Berg, "Rater to Add Policyholder Panic Factor," *New York Times*, August 2, 1991.

[65]In the case of Mutual of New York, for example, $9.8 billion of its $14 billion in liabilities can be withdrawn on demand or on short notice. See Hylton, "MONY, Sorely Tested, Reassures Customers."

[66]See Berg, "Rater to Add Policyholder Panic Factor."

The only suitable lender of last resort at either the state or the federal level is the Federal Reserve Board. There are no state agencies with sufficient capitalization to provide this kind of liquidity assistance. The Federal Reserve, moreover, performs a similar lender-of-last-resort function for the banking industry.

In suggesting that the Federal Reserve perform this function, we wish to emphasize that the loans should truly be a matter of last resort. Even if authorized to provide liquidity assistance to insurance firms, the Fed should not do so unless it appears that all other feasible sources of funds have evaporated. Further, the Fed should provide lender-of-last-resort financing only for temporary liquidity assistance to solvent firms. In no event should federal assistance be provided to insolvent firms.

Thus, any temporary liquidity assistance should be fully secured by collateral. In most cases, such collateral would be readily available in the form of privately placed debt that cannot be liquidated quickly at market rates but that nevertheless has collateral value. Moreover, before the Fed intervenes with assistance, it should receive a certification from the insurance commissioner of the firm's domicile that the firm is not insolvent. In addition, the relevant state guaranty funds might be required to bear a substantial amount of the insolvency risk by means of agreements to indemnify the Fed in the event that the emergency loans are not repaid and the collateral proves insufficient to satisfy the shortfall.

With these safeguards in place, the Fed should have adequate assurance of prompt repayment when it advances temporary liquidity assistance. Accordingly, we do not believe that this assistance by the Federal Reserve needs to be accompanied by any other form of federal solvency regulation.

5
Rate Regulation

WE NOW TURN TO THE FINAL major topic of this volume, that of rate regulation. Aside from solvency regulation, the various mechanisms for setting, or participating in the setting, of insurance rates, as well as for policing against deviations from filed rates through rebating and like devices, constitute the other major prong of state insurance regulation.

These systems of rate setting are anomalous. Insurance is the only major industry in the United States that is both highly unconcentrated—almost all markets are served by a large number of firms, with no firm controlling enough of the market to exercise market power—and yet subject to price controls in many states. This chapter describes the state rate-setting regimes and then considers the arguments for and against rate regulation, as well as the impact of proposed federal solvency regulation on state rate-setting programs. We conclude that insurance rates should be set by market forces and not by any form of governmental regulation.[1]

State Insurance Commissions

The states adopt two general approaches to rate setting, each with several variants.[2] Most states—approximately thirty in the case of property and casualty insurance—follow the traditional practice[3] of

---

[1]Our conclusion in this regard is consistent with the recommendations of a number of earlier studies, including the American Enterprise Institute's 1977 study, see MacAvoy, ed., *Federal-State Regulation of the Pricing and Marketing of Insurance*, p. 89, concluding that "rigid state rate regulation has had adverse effects" and that "vigorous competition is consistent with the goal of reasonable rates."

[2]State power to control rates was upheld by the Supreme Court in 1914, German Alliance Insurance Co. v. Lewis, 233 U.S. 389 (1914), and has not been seriously questioned since.

[3]The system of prior state approval of rates is recommended in the NAIC's "All

requiring that rates be approved in advance by the regulator.[4] In a few states, such as Massachusetts, the regulator sets the rate; in others, the regulator reviews a rate filed by the insurance company itself or by an independent insurance rating bureau.[5] One typical pattern (sometimes referred to as "flex rating") is for the state to define a range in which rates can fluctuate from a defined base line. In practice, many state systems allow for considerable deviation from the filed rates. Commercial filings in some states, for example, can legally be modified by as much as 70 percent.[6] Actual rates rarely deviate this much from the filed rates, but in volatile markets they may sometimes change by as much as 50 percent from previous rates.[7]

The remaining states—40 percent in the case of property and casualty firms—do not require prior approval of rates but rather allow rates to be set by market forces (in theory, at least).[8] Most of these states require that rates be filed before or soon after use and retain the power to reject rates deemed unfair, unreasonable, or excessive.[9] The stringency of this *post hoc* review process varies from state to state. Some states, such as Illinois, provide only minimal state oversight, relying on market forces to ensure the fairness of rates.[10] Others exercise more vigorous oversight.

Over the past few years, state rate-setting activity has become controversial as a result of consumer-oriented reforms of two general types: rate rollbacks and structural reform of rate making.

Industry" model statute, promulgated in 1945 at the time of the enactment of the McCarran-Ferguson Act. See Gastel, *Rate Regulation.*

[4]See Insurance Information Institute, *1990 Property/Casualty Insurance Facts.*

[5]See Gastel, *Rate Regulation.*

[6]See Gerald D. Stephens, "Please, No More Complaints," *Best's Review,* vol. 91, no. 9 (1991), p. 61.

[7]See ibid.

[8]States began to adopt these competitive rate-setting programs in the 1970s. See Gastel, *Rate Regulation.* It should be noted that Proposition 103 represents a return to the older system of prior approval, albeit with a view toward benefiting consumers rather than insurance firms.

[9]See Insurance Information Institute, *1990 Property/Casualty Insurance Fact Book,* p. 13.

[10]See Stephens, "Please, No More Complaints."

Rate Rollbacks. Some states have intervened dramatically to hold down rates in particularly sensitive lines, such as automobile insurance.[11] The most prominent recent example of state consumer legislation is California's Proposition 103, approved by that state's voters on November 8, 1988.[12] Proposition 103 repealed the state antitrust exemption for insurance firms as well as its antirebate law, required advance administrative approval for rates, allowed banks to sell insurance, required an immediate 20 percent reduction in automobile, homeowner, commercial, and municipal liability rates, and froze rate increases for a year subject to a limited waiver for cases where the insurer could establish that it was substantially threatened with insolvency.

Pennsylvania also adopted automobile insurance reform legislation in 1990. The Pennsylvania law required rollbacks of 22 percent for policyholders accepting restrictions on lawsuits and 10 percent for those wanting to take advantage of the tort system in the event of an accident.[13]

Most recently, Texas adopted comprehensive insurance reform. Although the Texas legislation contains many "proconsumer" features, it does not opt for stringent rate regulation as under California's Proposition 103. On the contrary, the Texas law deregulated a number of lines, including general liability and commercial property insurance, which are now subject to a file-and-use requirement with no need for prior administrative approval.[14] Other lines, such as private passenger auto, commercial auto, and personal property insurance, are subject to more stringent regulation, but even for these lines a firm may file and use a rate, without prior approval, so long as it remains within a flex band of the administratively established benchmark rate.[15]

Structural Reforms. In addition to rate rollbacks, some states have

---

[11]Massachusetts regulators have reportedly been holding automobile insurance rates below market-clearing rates. See Muhl, "A Ceasefire in the War of Words," p. 28.

[12]Codified at Cal. Ins. Code § 1861.

[13]See Gastel, *Rate Regulation*.

[14]See Fayhee, "Texas Reforms Pass by Big Margin." Before the recent legislation, Texas was the only state other than Massachusetts that set uniform rates by administrative fiat.

[15]See ibid.

adopted structural reforms of their rate-making proceedings—changes that, in the long run, may have a greater impact than the more highly publicized rate rollbacks. One important structural reform has been the move toward popular election of state insurance commissioners. The goal of this reform is to make the state insurance commissioner more accountable to the public—and presumably more responsive to populist pressures—and less influenced by insurance industry lobbyists.

If recent experience in California is illustrative, this move to elected officials may affect insurance regulation in significant ways. Early in 1991, the newly elected insurance commissioner of that state, John Garamendi, received widespread publicity by announcing that capital not used to write business in California would henceforth be included in the rate base and indicating that he intended to rescind rate increases approved by his predecessor in office.[16] Garamendi vowed to "put bigger rollbacks in consumers' pockets and crack down on excessive rates in the future."[17] Consumer advocate Ralph Nader praised the new commissioner, observing that "because the former regime so arrogantly refused to enforce the will of the people, the new commissioner's responsibility is clear."[18] This kind of regulatory populism plays well at the ballot box and can be expected to occur more frequently as other states move toward elected insurance commissioners.

A second important structural reform has been to change the procedures for rate setting by giving consumer and public interest representatives explicit representation in rate-setting procedures. Texas, for example, now requires that a consumer advocate participate in such proceedings. California's Proposition 103 created a "consumer advocacy corporation" to represent consumer interests in insurance matters, but the California Supreme Court struck the provision down as a violation of the state constitution.[19]

Consumer legislation of this sort sometimes results in a transfer of wealth from insurance firms to consumers. A number of studies of

---

[16]See Wojcik, "New Regulator Freezes Rates under Prop 103."

[17]See ibid.

[18]Ibid.

[19]See Calfarm Insurance Co. v. Deukmejian, 771 P.2d 1247, 48 Cal. 3d 805, 258 Cal. Rptr. 161 (1989).

Proposition 103 have documented significant negative impacts on insurance company stock prices in the days surrounding the election in which Proposition 103 was adopted.[20] These wealth effects do not in themselves establish that Proposition 103 and like programs are undesirable as a matter of social policy. If insurance companies have been systematically overcharging, as consumer advocates claim, the rate rollbacks could actually increase the efficiency of insurance markets relative to the current system, although it is unlikely that administered rates of the sort now enforced in California would be more efficient than rates set by market forces. If, however, rates are set too low, there is an obvious threat to insurance company solvency. It is too early to say whether state legislation to roll back rates and other consumer-oriented laws actually threaten the solvency of insurance firms. It should be noted, however, that the A. M. Best Company has issued qualified ratings for firms exposed to the financial uncertainties of regulatory programs in California, New Jersey, Kentucky, Massachusetts, Michigan, New York, North Carolina, Pennsylvania, and South Carolina.[21]

Private Rating Organizations

However they are set—by administrative fiat, marketplace forces, or something in between—insurance rates necessarily reflect projections about expected losses, expenses, and profits. Information of this sort is gathered and analyzed by private underwriting organizations. The historical pattern is for these underwriting associations to issue advisory rates that reflect not only historical loss data but also assumptions about expenses and profits. These advisory rates, in turn, were often used to establish uniform industry rates, either by

---

[20]See Roger M. Cross and Mark L. Shelor, "Insurance Firm Market Response to California Proposition 103 and the Effects of Firm Size," *Journal of Risk and Insurance*, vol. 57 (1990), p. 682; Joseph A. Fields, Chinmoy Ghosh, David S. Kidwell, and Linda S. Klein, "Wealth Effects of Regulatory Reform: The Reaction to California's Propostion 103," *Journal of Financial Economics*, vol. 28 (1991), p. 233; Samuel H. Szewczyk and Raj Varma, "The Effect of Proposition 103 on Insurers: Evidence from the Capital Market," *Journal of Risk and Insurance*, vol. 57 (1990), p. 671.

[21]See Paul E. Wish, "Review and Preview: 1990 and 1991," *Best's Review*, vol. 91, no. 9 (1991), p. 14.

way of administrative mandate or through the operation of private cartels. It was just such an underwriting association-cartel that precipitated the Supreme Court's decision in *United States v. South-Eastern Underwriters Association*, which declared that insurance was subject to federal regulation and which in turn spawned the McCarran-Ferguson Act.[22]

For many years after the enactment of the McCarran-Ferguson Act in 1945, private rating organizations operated throughout the industry, almost always issuing advisory rates. As the insurance industry became increasingly national in scope and as firms entered multiple lines of coverage, the rating bureaus consolidated. Today there are two major rating bureaus in the property and casualty field, the Insurance Services Office, which provides advisory, actuarial, statistical, rating, and other services for property and casualty firms, including the preparation of policy forms; and the National Council on Compensation Insurance, which develops rating plans and systems for workers' compensation systems. A variety of statewide or specialized rating bureaus also remain in operation.

The degree to which advisory rates induce parallelism in pricing is not entirely clear. It would appear that firms deviate from advisory rates more frequently during unusual market conditions than at other times, that the larger firms are more likely to deviate than smaller or regional firms, and that greater variation occurs in commercial lines than in personal lines. Consumer advocates and others charge that advisory rates are little more than a thinly disguised continuation of the old system of cartelization through rating bureaus, which once prevailed in fire and other property and casualty lines. Industry advocates respond that there is plenty of competition in the industry, including price competition, as illustrated by the flexibility that individual firms currently enjoy over rates.

In recent years, the activities of these rate-setting organizations have become particularly controversial, owing to a number of discrete factors:

• The ability of private rating organizations to enforce the rates they issue has been seriously undermined, at least in the Ninth Circuit, by the decision in *In Re Insurance Antitrust Litigation*.[23]

---

[22]322 U.S. 533 (1944).

[23]See In re Insurance Antitrust Litigation, 938 F.2d 919 (9th Cir. 1991), cert.

• A number of states have acted affirmatively to reduce the power of the private rating organizations or even to eliminate them entirely. Many states now prohibit insurers doing business in the state from writing premiums based on a rating organization's advisory rate, requiring instead that only historical loss data be used. Thus, some rating organizations have resorted to providing two sorts of information: loss costs in states that prohibit the use of advisory rates and the traditional advisory rates in states that allow them.[24]

• Private insurance-rating organizations are introducing fundamental changes in the nature and form of the information they provide their insurance company clients.[25] The most important such change involved the Insurance Services Office, which announced in April 1989 that it planned to cease issuing advisory rates—which insurance companies could then file with their state regulators for approval—and would substitute advisory prospective loss costs.[26] The prospective loss cost does not set forth a recommended rate but rather provides data on prospective claims and the costs of claims handling. Non-claim–related information is excluded. Consumer advocates have charged that the advisory prospective loss costs are really recommended rates in disguise, since firms can extrapolate the recommended rates.[27] The ISO, however, contends that it will not provide trended expense data to insurance firms, but only historical aggregate expense information, devoid of actuarial analysis, projection, or judgment.[28]

---

granted sub nom. Hartford Fire Insurance Co. v. California, 113 S.Ct. 52 (1992).

[24]See Meg Fletcher, "NCCI to Shift Focus to Loss Costs," *Business Insurance*, July 23, 1990, p. 1. As of 1990, twenty-three states and the District of Columbia used fully developed advisory workers' compensation rates, while fourteen used a loss-cost approach; the remainder used other methods.

[25]These private initiatives, while voluntary in some sense, occurred in response to developments such as the enactment of California's Proposition 103 and the campaign in Congress to repeal the McCarran-Ferguson Act. See, for example, ibid., p. 1, reporting remarks by head of rating organization that move to loss costs was intended to "remove a lot of the rhetorical heat from the issue and help to calm the regulatory and legislative environment."

[26]See Lisa S. Howard, "ISO: No More Advisory Rates," *National Underwriter*, April 10, 1989, p. 1.

[27]See statement of J. Robert Hunter, president, National Insurance Consumer Organization, in H.R. 9 Hearings.

[28]See Howard, "ISO," p. 1.

The ISO's move away from advisory rates is likely to be mirrored by most or all of the important private rating organizations. The NAIC approved a recommendation in June 1989 to bar distribution of "final rates" by private rate-making bureaus in all lines except workers' compensation.[29] And the nation's largest workers' compensation insurance rating organization, the National Council on Compensation Insurance, announced in July 1990 that it was changing its focus from advisory rates to developed loss costs.[30] The new rates would include historical loss data but not allocations for insurer profits or underwriting expenses.[31]

Market Forces

The traditional argument in favor of state rate regulation is that state control over rates is necessary to protect consumers.[32] The argument has two main strands: first, that by virtue of their power and superior bargaining position, insurance companies are likely to overcharge consumers unless the state controls the permissible rates and, second, that insurance contracts are highly complex instruments that are difficult for consumers to understand and compare. Although these arguments are often lumped together, they are conceptually distinct: the first is premised on bargaining power, and the second is based on information costs. In one form or another, these are the principal justifications for rate regulation heard today.

These arguments are unpersuasive as a justification for state rate regulation. There is little reason to suppose that the state can do a better job than the market at setting rates. Insurance rates, like

---

[29]See Insurance Information Institute, *1990 Property/Casualty Insurance Facts*, p. 9.

[30]See Fletcher, "NCCI to Shift Focus to Loss Costs, Business Insurance."

[31]See ibid. The organization, however, would continue to provide developed rates to states that request them.

[32]Historically, rate regulation entered the insurance business during the populist era of the early twentieth century. Many states, over the vigorous opposition of the insurance industry, asserted the power to set rates and used that power to force insurance companies to lower the rates that they had previously been charging. Kansas and Texas enacted the first rate-regulation statutes in 1909 and quickly decreed reductions in insurance rates. See H. Roger Grant, *Insurance Reform: Consumer Action in the Progressive Era* (Ames, Iowa: State University Press, 1979).

other prices, should be set by market forces under conditions of free competition.

Any system of administered rates carries with it serious dangers of marketplace distortions. This potential exists regardless of whether rates are rolled back—as is happening in California and other states with consumer reform legislation on the books—or maintained at excessively high rates to enrich the coffers of insurance firms. We have already discussed the harm to consumers and the economic distortions that inevitably flow from a system of administered rates that deviate from market-clearing levels.

Some consumer advocates may believe that a return to administered prices, such as that seen recently in California, ensures that prices will not be set too high. But if the history of insurance regulation is a guide, populist revolts against insurance pricing rarely endure for long. Many states adopted price regulation during the populist revolt of the early twentieth century, and the initial experience under these systems was unfavorable to the insurance industry. Over time, however, the industry established influence over all or nearly all state insurance commissions; and before long the power to administer prices was being used to approve and enforce rates set by industry rating bureaus that operated, at the time at least, as little more than well-organized cartels.[33] When the fervor of the current populist revolt over insurance rates dies down—as it inevitably will—the industry may well be able to reassert its power and even to turn administered pricing systems to its own advantage.[34]

In addition to the market distortions and shortages caused by state rate regulation, there are the costs of administering such systems to consider. Although in the scheme of things, these costs

---

[33]This story of industry regulation is well documented in the standard histories of the industry, most notably H. Roger Grant's *Insurance Reform*. See also Morton Keller, *The Life Insurance Enterprise, 1885–1910* (Cambridge, Mass.: Belknap Press of Harvard University Press, 1963). Grant and other historians, however, miss many of the implications of their own evidence because of their failure to appreciate the importance of cartels in the development of the industry in the period they study.

[34]The danger of cartelization under the guise of rate setting is somewhat reduced by the structural reforms, discussed earlier, which attempt to impose a political check on industry capture of state insurance commissions. Such structural reforms may have an impact, but whether they will endure as effective checks on capture in the long run remains to be seen.

are fairly small—Proposition 103 reportedly added $25 million to the budget of California's insurance department[35]—they are not insignificant and suggest another, albeit marginal, reason for not imposing a system of administered price regulation on this highly competitive industry.

State-administered rates might have some appeal if it could be shown that private market forces would not work effectively to set appropriate rates. There is no evidence, however, that if suitable antitrust protections were in place, the industry would not set rates at efficient levels. Such evidence as exists suggests the contrary. Illinois, which went to free-market rate setting for most lines in 1971, has experienced no serious difficulties with rates. Premiums in Illinois for automobile and homeowners insurance are substantially lower than those in other industrial metropolitan states.[36]

The insurance industry seems ideally suited to rate setting by competitive forces. As economist Paul Joskow has observed:

> The property-liability insurance industry possesses the structural characterictics normally associated with the idealized competitive market: a large number of firms, operating in a market with low concentration levels, selling essentially identical products, provided at constant unit costs and with ease of entry of new and potential competitors. . . . It is . . . difficult to find . . . many other industries which conform more closely to the economist's idealized competitive market structure.[37]

Joskow's comments about the property and liability industry apply equally well to the life insurance industry: in that industry too are many producers selling very similar products. Based on these observations about industry structure, Joskow suggests that insurance rates

---

[35]See Stamp, "A Modest Proposal," p. 45.

[36]See ibid. An earlier study, however, found no evidence for the proposition that rates for automobile insurance would be higher in states with prior approval laws than in states without prior approval laws. Pauline Ippolito, "The Effects of Price Regulation in the Automobile Insurance Industry," *Journal of Law and Economics*, vol. 22 (1979), p. 55.

[37]Paul Joskow, "Cartels, Competition and Regulation in the Property-Liability Insurance Industry," *Bell Journal of Economics and Management Science*, vol. 4 (1973), pp. 375, 391.

and rating classifications should not be regulated at all:

> There are no natural monopoly characteristics which would indicate that open competition would be unstable and eventually lead to monopoly. Rather, the argument has been that rate making in concert through rating bureaus is a necessity to insure the public and the industry against "destructive" competition and large numbers of bankruptcies. There does not seem to be any reason why this industry should be more unstable than others.[38]

Consumer groups may seek state rate regulation because they see state regulations as a means for rolling back rates and accomplishing other policy objectives. Insurance regulators may favor rate regulation because they perceive that increased state control over rates will expand their powers, their budgets, and their political standing. And insurance companies may favor rate regulation as a shield against the antitrust laws. A potent political coalition in favor of enhanced state rate regulation might well develop.

Increased state involvement with rate setting would not be a constructive development because imposed rates are unlikely to be market-clearing rates. Instead, they would reflect alignments of political power within a given state. At times when "consumer" interests are strong, the rates are likely to be set below the market-clearing rates, resulting in losses to insurance companies and in distortions in the production of insurance products.[39] At other times, when industry groups are more powerful, rates are likely to be set too high; the result would again be wealth-reducing distortions in insurance markets because too little insurance would be purchased. Neither of these results would be desirable from the standpoint of consumers or the general public.

Our conclusion, in short, is that states should not set rates for insurance products. This does not mean, however, that the *federal* government *should* set rates. As uneconomical as state rate setting is

---

[38]Ibid., pp. 375, 423.

[39]The short-term consequence of rates set below the market-clearing rate would likely be the excessive purchasing of insurance by persons wishing to take advantage of the below-market rates. In the long term, however, the result would be likely to be underproduction of insurance as firms leave the market to avoid incurring additional losses.

likely to be, federal rate setting is likely to be worse, since it would be very difficult, at the federal level, to take account of regional or local conditions that affect the profitability of different insurance products. Neither the states nor the federal government should set insurance rates.

This conclusion suggests that in an ideal world the federal government would adopt legislation not only disclaiming any purpose to set rates itself but also preempting state efforts to set rates administratively. We do not recommend preemptive federal legislation at this time, both because the need for it is not yet clearly established and because corrective forces acting in the private sector may be sufficient to head off any major return to rate regulation by individual states.

We do recommend, however, a more limited federal preemption of state regulatory authority. As already noted, the threat that rates will be set too low has been checked, historically, by the ability of insurance firms to exit markets that become unattractive because of adverse regulatory policies. The recently implemented exit fees that deter firms from leaving markets in response to state regulatory initiatives undermine longstanding marketplace checks against state expropriation of insurance industry assets. In the long run, they may well harm consumers (by reducing the supply of insurance), undermine industry solvency, and spark an unhealthy competition in which states vie to set unrealistically low rates to benefit their own citizens at the expense of the national interest. The problem of exit fees is serious enough to warrant a limited preemption to prohibit states from penalizing any firm that elects either to leave a state altogether or to leave any line of insurance within a state, when the firm's decision is based on economic factors and is not part of any boycott or cooperative enterprise to pressure the state to alter its regulations.

There is little justification for allowing states to lock insurance firms within their borders. Exit fees do not serve the values of federalism—that is, offering firms a choice of locations in which to do business. On the contrary, they eliminate one of the principal mechanisms by which corporations are protected against burdensome state regulation.

6

Conclusion

THIS STUDY HAS EXAMINED the arguments for and against the McCarran-Ferguson Act in today's marketplace and regulatory environment. We conclude that the boycott exception to the McCarran-Ferguson Act should be interpreted to permit vigorous enforcement against industry practices that suppress or threaten to suppress competition. Similarly, state action immunity should be limited to situations in which the activities in question are both endorsed by state legislation or regulation, and not merely permitted as a matter of administrative practice or authorized by implication, and subject to active, continuous, and meaningful state oversight. At the same time, there are good arguments for retaining the antitrust immunity for a fairly wide range of cooperative activities within the industry, including the compilation and dissemination of historical loss costs and the production of nonexclusive standardized forms and policies, as well as prospective loss cost analysis that does not facilitate the development of agreements among firms on rates. It may be useful to formulate explicit safe-harbor legislation to protect these cooperative activities if the McCarran-Ferguson Act is repealed or revised by Congress, or interpreted by the judiciary, in such a way as to raise questions about the legality under federal antitrust laws of such legitimate cooperative activities.

We do not believe it is appropriate at this time to institute federal solvency regulation. Despite recent failures, the insurance industry is not now undergoing a solvency crisis, and the general performance of state insurance regulators at safeguarding insurance company solvency has been good—in contrast with the abysmal failure of federal banking regulators to ensure the solvency of that industry. Limited federal involvement through an interstate compact might, however, be a useful means for rationalizing and coordinating state regulatory programs.

We conclude that there are no good arguments for government control over rates in this highly unconcentrated, competitive industry. Rates should be set by market forces. In light of the trend among the states toward market rate setting, which has only recently been interrupted by an unfortunate regression toward administered rates in several states, we conclude that the time is not yet ripe for preemptive federal regulation displacing state authority over insurance rates. We do recommend, however, that the federal government preempt state lock-in rules that penalize firms wishing to exit a state altogether or to cease offering a line of insurance within a state, when the firm's decision to leave rests on economic considerations and is not part of any plan to boycott a state to pressure regulators to change their regulations.

The insurance industry is now undergoing enormous marketplace and regulatory strains. It is our hope that this volume will contribute to the study of the industry and to the appropriate resolution of its problems.

About the Authors

JONATHAN R. MACEY is the J. DuPratt White Professor of Law at Cornell University and director of the John M. Olin Program in Law and Economics at Cornell Law School. He specializes in corporate law, banking regulation, law and economics, and the economics of regulation. Professor Macey has written three books, more than seventy scholarly articles, and a number of editorials for such publications as the *Wall Street Journal* and the *Los Angeles Times*.

Professor Macey is the reporter for the American Bar Association's Committee on Corporate Laws' Model Business Corporation Act revision project, the president elect of the Association of American Law Schools' section on Financial Institutions and Consumer Financial Services, associate editor of the *Journal of Legal Education*, a member of the board of arbitrators of the National Association of Securities Dealers, and a member of the Executive Committee of the AALS section on corporate law.

He has taught at the law schools at Emory University, the University of Virginia, the University of Chicago, and the University of Tokyo. He graduated from Harvard College and received his law degree from the Yale Law School.

GEOFFREY P. MILLER is the Kirkland & Ellis Professor of Law at the University of Chicago Law School. His areas of particular interest are financial institutions, law and economics, and the separation of powers. His work focuses on the complex tensions and interactions among four fundamental social systems: politics, markets, technology, and law. He is the author of two books and more than fifty scholarly articles and a hundred shorter pieces. His articles have appeared in the *Columbia Law Review*, the *University of Chicago Law Review*, the *Journal of Legal Studies*, the *Stanford Law Review*, the *Yale Law Journal,* and elsewhere.

Professor Miller received his B.A. magna cum laude from Princeton University in 1973 and a J.D. from Columbia Law School in 1978. Before joining the University of Chicago faculty in 1983, he served as a law clerk to two federal judges, including Supreme Court Justice Byron White, was an attorney-adviser in the Justice Department's Office of Legal Counsel, and worked in a private law firm in Washington, D.C.